Jack Ransom, a ninety-three-year-old World War II veteran, lives with his eighty-two-year-old wife Maddie in the Ayrshire seaside town of Largs.

At the age of ninety he mastered the computer to write the story of his eventful life. Born in Peckham to working class parents, his youth was spent in Deptford and Greenwich. During the war he was captured by the Japanese at Singapore.

After the war, employment and marriage was initially found in Scotland, but life had its difficulties. Recently Jack has given talks to Rotary Clubs, Round Tables, and Church Groups.

The Scottish Cockney

**Jack Ransom**

# The Scottish Cockney

Olympia Publishers
*London*

**www.olympiapublishers.com**
OLYMPIA PAPERBACK EDITION

A CIP catalogue record for this title is
available from the British Library.

ISBN: 978-1-84897-430-2

Every effort has been made to trace copyright ownership and to obtain
permission for reproduction of the maps printed in this book. If you believe
you are the copyright owner of either of these maps, and we have not
requested your permission, please contact us.

**First Published in 2014**

Olympia Publishers
60 Cannon Street
London
EC4N 6NP

Printed in Great Britain

I dedicate this book to the memory of my comrades who did not return home, and are buried either in Thailand or Burma. We who came back will remember them until we are also gone.

# Acknowledgments

Producing this book at the age of ninety-three has not been easy, and learning to use a laptop computer in addition to researching my memory had its difficulties. Without my friends (particularly those in Cumbrae Court, Largs) who listened to me reminiscing and uttered those fateful words 'you should write a book' it would never have been written. Many have given advice regarding problems that came up, for which I am extremely grateful. In particular I am indebted to my nephew's wife Elsa Reid, who wishes to be known as my 'acting unpaid literary agent'!

To be more serious, I am extremely obliged to Rod Beattie at the Thailand-Burma Railway Centre in Kanchanaburi, Thailand for the use of photographs in connection with the construction of the Railway. He, along with others are doing invaluable work in preserving the history of the Railway, for which we should be forever grateful. Finally I would mention my dear wife Maddie, whose support and understanding was always there in the preparation of my book.

# Contents

# Foreword

By Chris Koster,
Attorney General of Missouri

As improbable as it may seem, I met Jack Ransom in a bar in Bangkok in the fall of 2009.

I had never met him before, and I have never met him since.

But there is a picture of Jack that hangs prominently in my office, and I'll never forget our conversation as long as I live.

Jack was around ninety-years-old when we met, but he was young: his eyes were young, mischievous, and happy. And he smiled easily. Oh, it was impossible not to like him.

And he was a storyteller.

In the Bamboo Bar, in the old Oriental Hotel, just metres from the Chao Phraya River, Jack Ransom unpacked the magical tale of his life.

It was the story of a young Englishmen in the late 1930s, enlisted in His Majesty's Service at the onslaught of World War II. It was the story of a boy-soldier who proposed to a beautiful, young British girl just days before shipping off to the vicious dangers of the South Pacific, where he would soon be taken prisoner by the Japanese, marched for five years through Southeast Asia, and pressed into forced labour as his fellow prisoners of war died of wretched disease – and worse.

It was the story of the Great War ending, prisoners released, and this man-soldier, shrunken from malnutrition, returning to England to find the girl he had proposed to years before. It was the story of how she stood waiting for him on a dock in post-war London, as thousands upon thousands of changed men – in uniforms that no longer fit – disembarked their battleships.

It was a love story about losing a woman after loving her for thirty years, and believing love would never come again, but then finding another woman and loving her for thirty years too… and then losing for a second time.

And then love's rebirth.

It was the story of an old man, young at heart, widowed twice over, boarding by himself the luxurious and infamous Orient Express. More than sixty years after his release from a Japanese prison camp, Jack Ransom would return to Southeast Asia to retrace the prisoner's journey he had taken long ago at the point of a bayonet. But this time, his journey would be five-star – an unmistakable middle finger to the ghosts of the past.

It was an epic story of an optimistic old man, with young, mischievous, and enduring eyes.

That night in Bangkok, Jack Ransom talked. I listened in awe and wonder. Even now, thinking of Jack can make my eyes well up… with extraordinary respect for a life so well-lived.

So pour two fingers of scotch, sit back, and relive a heroic British tale of love and courage, optimism, and endurance.

February 2014

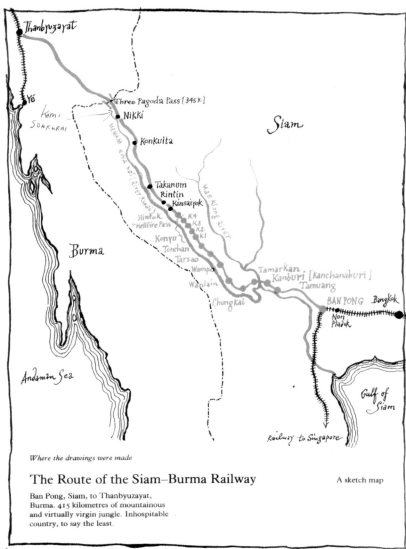

Thanbyuzayat

Yé

Kami
Sonkurai

Three Pagoda Pass [345 k.]

Nikki

Konkuita

Siam

Menam Kwa Noi (River Kwei)

Takanum
Rintin
Kinsaiyok

Hintok
"Hellfire Pass"

K4
K3
K2
K1

Konyu
Tonchan

Wae Klong River

Tarsao

Wampo

Wanlain

Tamarkan
Kanburi [Kanchanaburi]
Tamuang

Chungkai

BAN PONG    Bangkok

Nom
Pladuk

Burma

Andaman Sea

Gulf of
Siam

Railway to Singapore

*Where the drawings were made*

## The Route of the Siam–Burma Railway

A sketch map

Ban Pong, Siam, to Thanbyuzayat,
Burma. 415 kilometres of mountainous
and virtually virgin jungle. Inhospitable
country, to say the least.

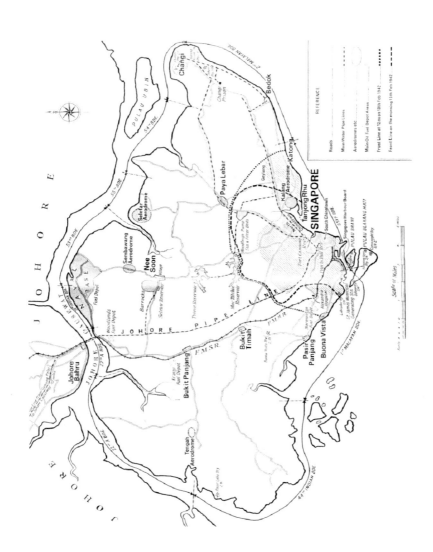

# The Early Years

## 1920–1937: Childhood to Grammar School

Her Majesty Queen Mary wife of King George V gazed down at the two infants that had been presented to her by Margaret McMillan and was intrigued to learn that she was being introduced to an aunt and her nephew. The occasion was the visit of her Majesty to the nursery school opened by the McMillan sisters in 1914 for the benefit of the children of Deptford London. This visit by the Queen was in the early 1920s and was recorded by a local newspaper reporter. Among my earliest memories I can recall that in the parlour of my grandmother's terraced house there was a framed reproduction of a newspaper photograph depicting the event, but except for that one occasion I never saw the photograph again. It is possible that it disappeared during enemy bombing in the Second World War I am fairly certain that the two infants were Nelly Carr my mother's youngest sister and me. I believe I was placed in the nursery school at about the age of three when my parents moved from Camberwell to live in a small terraced house in Creek Road Deptford.

I cannot recall the Queen speaking to me but I certainly remember being at the school, my main memory being put to sleep on a rough canvas bed in the afternoon, out in the open come winter or summer, come rain or shine. Now that I am at the age of ninety-three it does not seem to have done me much harm! My father was Frederick Charles Ransom and he married my mother Elizabeth Rosina Carr in June 1919 presumably after his return from the great War and in the following year I was born on 15 April 1920 in the Peckham district of Camberwell (immortalised in modern television sitcoms as Del boy country) and christened Robert John but was always known in the family as Jack which puzzled me for several years until I learned that I had been named after my father's younger brother Robert John who had been killed on 28 March 1918 whilst serving with the London Rifles and that he had always been known by his nickname of Jack. Apparently he had only joined the forces in the previous year so like many he was only a teenager who died in the aftermath of the Great War. Jack was one of the many casualties arising from the German's last desperate push of the war, namely the battle of Arras. History records that following the stopping of the German offensive the Allies with the aid of tanks moved forward to attack the Hindenburg line leading eventually to the armistice. The newly born following the war were often named after members of the family that had been killed, I have no doubt that my father really missed his young teenage brother.

I think that you will gather from the initial paragraph that my maternal grandmother had a very large family. It would seem from records that possibly three sons were killed in the Great War and possibly two or three children died in infancy, and as I knew of three surviving sons and three daughters my grandparent's family on my mother's side numbered into double figures. There is no doubt that my granny Carr had a hard life despite which she reached an age well into her nineties; they say that longevity comes from your maternal grandparents so I have a lot to thank them for. My grandfather,

Tom Carr, skippered in his later years a Thames barge named the Director which he sailed from the canal in Camberwell through the then Surrey Commercial docks into the Thames and along to the north Kent coast to bring back a cargo of chalk, the bulk of which I understood was used in the whitening of the front steps of London houses. Maybe my leg was being pulled regarding this piece of information. Probably its use was more industrial, for example in the production of talcum powder.

My grandfather had with him on his trips his son, my uncle Harry who in his spare time was a very useful amateur boxer. Sailing down the Thames and back often against the prevailing wind and dodging the numerous Tugs and Steamships which were entering and leaving the numerous docks on the Thames must have been very tricky at times. Sometimes if the tide was against them they would anchor just off the coal wharf at Greenwich, come ashore and pop in for a meal with us till the tide turned. The Coal wharf at Greenwich as far as I know is now a pier for river taxis landing people at the Millennium Dome. As a young boy I worshipped my uncle Harry, his ability as an amateur boxer certainly helped but on one occasion he probably saved my life. One Saturday morning I went with him down to the barge which had been tied up the previous night in the canal at Camberwell to clean it out and do one or two necessary jobs. This was a great adventure for me after a week of humdrum life at school, and after completing the chores we made our way homewards back along the tow path. My uncle strode ahead but I lingered to watch some lads further up the canal fishing while at the same time I walked backwards and straight into the canal. I couldn't swim at that time and I believe I was going down for the third time when my uncle realised I was no longer with him. Needless to say he pulled me out and we went back to the barge to dry off. Before we arrived home my uncle told me in no uncertain terms was I to let my mother know of the incident as, in his words "she will kill me for not looking after you".

I learned later in life that my mother as one of the oldest in the family, could as you might say, put the fear of death in the remainder of her brothers and sisters. Uncle Harry had several bouts during his boxing career and I remember him telling me of an occasion when he met a policeman in a 10 round bout at Goldsmiths College London and invited his father Tom Carr (my grandfather) to watch him fight. This proved to be a mistake as during the fight he was distracted by his father standing on his seat shouting instructions and pleading him "to kill" his opponent much to the horror of the gentlemen spectators watching an amateur bout. You will gather that my grandfather was not a great lover of the Metropolitan police force!

During Bank holidays the Showmen came to the fairground on Blackheath and in those days one of the shows was the boxing booth, needless to say this was a great attraction as the proprietor of the booth would offer a prize of two or three pounds for anyone to go three rounds with one of the boxers in his stable. In most cases when the challenge was taken up by a member of the audience he only lasted a minute or two when faced by a wily old professional. Harry, not being paid a great deal by his father was happy to take the chance of earning a a pound or two and at most times managed to collect the prize-money. Of course when the booth promoters got to know him they tended if possible to ignore his challenge, in those days a pound was a lot of money to them. You will have realised by now that uncle Harry meant a great deal to me and I was always over the moon when I was allowed to visit him and his wife Gert at his flat in the New Kent Road where he would get the boxing gloves out and we would engage in a mock fight with Harry kneeling on the floor to be the right height for me.

An additional attraction in the parlour was his Mynah bird which was a great source of amusement with its vocabulary of words and sayings which were added to from time to time. Gert would sometimes say to the bird "who is a lovely boy?" to which the reply would come "your Harry is a lovely boy", but of course if Harry was in the Black book the question and the answer was completely different and not suitable for my young ears. Harry was a great storyteller, some of his stories may not have been true but he did tell me that he had served on a ship laying transatlantic cables. I think he said its name was the Dominion and on one occasion during very heavy weather in the Atlantic he had been saved from going overboard by a close relative who was also a shipmate and that later on in life that person (who had died some years previously) paid him a visit. Harry reckoned that on getting a knock at the front door and opening it, the relative had entered walked past him up the hall and simply disappeared. The story was a little hard to believe bearing in mind the boxing career, maybe Harry had been on the end of too many punches!

There is no doubt in my mind that my uncle Harry lived quite an eventful life. I know that one or two occasions in order to make a little money he loaded up a barrow with cockles, mussels and shrimps (obtained from Billingsgate market) and sold the produce on a Sunday afternoon at 3 p.m. outside local public houses when they closed. Trade was good; customers going home for Sunday lunch probably required a peace offering when they arrived in a jolly mood! In later years in the war, of course I was not in touch with Harry but I believe that he took up the job of being a blacksmith and in that capacity he was employed fitting guns to merchant ships for their defence.

Later on in life before he went to live the final years of his life in Banbury Harry had a job at the New Cross Palais de Dance as a doorman, when on numerous occasions being handy with his fists he was called upon to bring about peace on a Saturday night, but I am sure knowing him as a gentle man he carried out his duties with decorum. He has been dead now for many years but I still remember him, his smile, and his lovable nature, with affection.

My grandfather Tom Carr in spite of his hard life with the barge was also a very gentle man (except when Harry needed backup) who did not drink or smoke and at the weekend he liked nothing better than to sit down with a cup of tea and play cribbage with anyone he could persuade to play with him. I normally went with my mother to visit her parents on a Friday night and sure enough the cribbage board was brought out and I was summoned to sit down and play. If I say so myself I became quite expert and we enjoyed many a game until my parents moved in 1935 from Deptford to Eltham in the London suburbs, nevertheless I played the occasional game with him up to the declaration of war in 1939. I did not see him again until my return from the Far East at the end of 1945, when sadly he had lost his sight and the cribbage games were no more. When I went down to see him just before Christmas that year on my return home, he was very emotional, he made sure for himself that my arms and legs were all complete, my verbal assurances were not enough for him. My dear grandfather Thomas William Carr died nine months later in Greenwich Hospital, I was left as a memento his moustache cup and saucer probably given to him by his wife on the occasion of their marriage in 1891 and maybe even at my age of ninety three I might try and grow a good bushy moustache and have a cup of tea without getting it wet!. My grandmother Elizabeth Rosina Carr lived on for at least another 20 years and died in a hospice in her late nineties.

Just a year or two before I left the nursery school at age six or seven my brother Fred was born and presumably also went to the nursery school; however I myself was enrolled at the elementary school further along Creek Road and was there until I reached age eleven. Creek Road elementary School for boys was set in Deptford, a very poor part of south-east London and there is no doubt we were a very rough set of lads with parents who in the main worked in unskilled jobs locally. Many of the lads could handle themselves physically and were not adverse to picking a fight with anyone including the teachers. One lad in particular, I remember his name was Dabin, a son of a costermonger and even at the age of ten had many a stand-up fight with a teacher whose name I remember was Easter, known to all the lads as Eggy. Needless to say the fight was egged on by all the class.

Round about the time when I left the nursery school and when radio or wireless was still more or less in its infancy, my father who had a crystal set, regularly tuned in to London 2LO an operation which in itself was very difficult owing to the vibration from the trams running outside, making the adjustment with the "cats whisker" extremely difficult. However on one occasion he handed me an earpiece and to my astonishment I heard a voice say, "This is uncle Mac, if Jackie goes upstairs and looks in the top drawer of his mother's dressing table he will find his birthday present." 93 years later that pleasurable moment is still with me. Returning to the four or five years I spent at the elementary school, looking back I still cannot believe how I learned enough to obtain a London County scholarship at the age of eleven. I think it was all due to one dedicated teacher and of course my father. In that year of 1931 myself and one other lad who obtained a free scholarship were the only ones to escape a future of leaving at age fourteen to find manual work locally.

The small terrace house we lived in was on Creek Road halfway between the school and Deptford Creek where there was a lifting bridge, following which the road went on into Church Street and the centre of Greenwich. It was a busy road with electric trams which took the current from a slot between the rails, eventually the tram route went on to Woolwich where the current was taken from overhead wires by means of a long pole. These trams were double deckers with the upper deck open at the ends and in those days the tram system extended over a great part of London until in a later decade the tracks were removed and trolley buses replaced the trams. When this took place it gave a distant relative named Spider Carr the opportunity to purchase the tarred blocks in which the rails had been set, then employ about four women to chop them up into bundles of sticks for fire lighting and sell them two bundles for three halfpennies. It was rumoured that he made a fortune, lived to the age of ninety-nine and died an unnatural death being knocked down crossing Church Street by a lorry, apparently going to his local pub for a midday pint. I always understood that the name of "Spider" was due to the manner of his walk, but of course I was only a youngster in those days, listening to talk in the family and of course Cockneys always tell a good story. As well as the trams buses also ran along Creek Road and I remember the early ones had solid tyres and were open on the top deck. On rainy days if you were unlucky to find the bottom deck full then you had no option but to go up to the top deck, unhook the rubber apron in front of your seat and cover your knees ; this kept your bottom half reasonably dry but of course the rest of you got soaked. I really did miss the trams as in my early teenage years I liked nothing better on a Saturday than to spend one shilling on an all-day ticket and tour as much of London as I could.

You will gather by now that Creek Road was quite busy as apart from the vehicle traffic there were several traders plying their wares. Salt and vinegar were sold from a barrow, milk was delivered from a large urn on a barrow, and muffins were also sold and carried on the head of the trader. The milk delivery required you to put out a metal can every morning to be filled and I especially remembered the salt, as the large lump which had been cut by a saw from a great block on the barrow, then sold to my mother, was given to me to break into two, then rubbed together so that at the end of my chore a nice pile of sifted salt was left. Across from our house was a small row of shops including a cafe which advertised itself as a good pull up for Carmen in other words for draymen with their horses and carts of which in those days there were many.

Creek Road led to the east to Greenwich which with its pier and Park was a great fascination to me, and to the West lay Deptford with its busy high Street which led up to the Broadway with its dance halls etc. Greenwich Park was a Mecca for small boys, great for exploration and picnics. During school holidays off I went with my younger brother equipped with our rations of sandwiches and lemonade spending the whole day in the park before returning at dusk. There was the added attraction of the observatory and the famous Zero longitude line marked on the pavement. In those days no one seemed to worry about you being missing for hours and I suppose my only irritation concerned my having to look after my brother who being five years younger than myself would insist on tagging along on all occasions. Deptford High Street was a fascinating place with its shops, the Electric Palace Cinema, the market, the station and the showground. On a Saturday morning, younger brother tagging along, we went to the cinema for the children's programme which needed each of us to have two pence for admission and there we watched the silent films of the day. These were normally cowboy films, sometimes Charlie Chaplin, and on occasion what were to us horror epics; all these were accompanied by an elderly lady thumping away on a upright piano. I remember to this day a film called "The Mummy" which gave my brother and I nightmares for a week. The showground was a blaze of colour and lights with the usual stalls and roundabouts which I really enjoyed until the occasion when I fell off my horse on the roundabout and was taken to the local clinic to be repaired, just a split lip and a bruise on my cheek. Also I still bear the scar on my chin following a Charlie Chaplin film when my brother later copied an episode in it and hit me with a hammer shouting " I'm Charlie", this meant another visit to the clinic but my brother I felt was left off lightly on account of his age!

Our house in Creek Road was a modest two up and two down terrace house with small front and back gardens, it still only had gas for lighting and cooking. Installation of electricity did not come along until the 1930s, and what was also basic was the outside toilet which had the added attraction of being back-to-back with the one next door. My brother and I shared the second bedroom and illumination came normally from a small gas mantle which being very fragile only lasted a day or two so it was dispensed with on account of cost and we made do with the fish tail burner. Our house was about a quarter of a mile from the school and to get to it we passed a major attraction, namely a sweet shop. The shop being close to the school had a considerable number of young clients; most of the boys popped in with their half pennies and were faced with a dilemma. On the shop counter was a cardboard box containing a stack of envelopes and on handing over your halfpenny you could take your pick and the envelope chosen would reveal whether you could have sweets to the value of one farthing or two pence, needless to say the latter very seldom turned up. Thinking about this in later years I am convinced that the shop owner retired as a millionaire, and that a high proportion of the youth of Deptford became addicted gamblers.

Deptford has an extremely interesting past history, Peter the Great of Russia had studied shipbuilding there, Samuel Pepys often visited in connection with his naval duties and the Creek may have been the scene when Sir Walter Raleigh laid down his cloak for the Tudor Queen Elizabeth to step upon; that last piece of information may just be my imagination but I reckon that the Creek must have been a great place to anchor a ship on its return to Greenwich after its long voyage.

My years at Creek Road School were fairly uneventful but I did study quite hard and as I remarked before I managed to win a junior county scholarship which gave my parents the choice of sending me at age eleven to one out of six Grammar schools in south-east London. The scholarship carried a bursary which helped my parents in providing school uniform etc and in order to cut out any cost of travel the nearest school namely the Addey and Stanhope was chosen, as I had also passed their entrance examination for a free place. Having progressed from a scruffy urchin to a passable young student I would now spend the next six years studying at the school situated in Deptford Broadway opposite the New Cross Empire.

The New Cross Empire, sadly no longer in existence conjures up for me many enjoyable memories as just before and for two or three years after I entered the grammar school my mother and I saw many great performances there. My mother was a great devotee of the music hall and as my father was more interested in the radio I went along with her to the first evening shows which normally started at 6.40 p.m., I found the lights, music and colour of performances absolutely fascinating. I can still recall Harry Tate and Company with their sketch called "Selling a car." Billy Bennett with his monologues, and who could forget "Call of the Yukon"? I also remember Billy Merson singing "The Spaniard that blighted my life" but more importantly I remember Gus Elliott who succeeded Eugene Stratton because he sang my mother's favourite song namely "Lily of Laguna", she was of course called Lily in the family. In later years whenever that song was played it always brought on the tears. We normally went to the first evening show on a Friday night and on one occasion we were sitting in the stalls when I was aware that a gigantic man had taken the seat next to me. I could see that he was dressed in a remarkable check suit, wore a red plastic nose and was wearing very heavy makeup. This I found very disconcerting even more so when he summoned over the usherette and purchased a large ice cream for me which I was happy to take, on getting the approval of my mother. At the end of the next act my companion was summoned to the stage and was introduced as everyone's favourite, the one and only," Harry Champion". We were then of course given a rendition of "Boiled Beef and Carrots" a song made famous by him. The older music hall acts later gave way to others such as "Flotsam and Jetsam", duet on piano, Albert Whelan, the whistler of song," Nat Mills and Bobby", comedians, and one of my favourites namely" Wilson, Keppel and Betty who were famous for their Egyptian dance routine. Sometimes after the finish of a Friday night performance at about 8.45 p.m. my mother and I would treat ourselves to supper on our way home, at the Pie and Eel shop in the High  Street, opposite the Cinema, and then in the words of Samuel Pepys "And so to bed"

It was at the beginning of September 1931 that I began attending the Addey and Stanhope school and my first two or three years passed by very rapidly, to a large extent in awe and bewilderment. I suppose that as a new boy it was a case of being seen and not heard and being a co-educational school the presence of girls added quite a bit to my early discomfort. I think that it was at the age of fourteen that I really began to notice the girls, along with the other lads we became aware that they were different from the waist upwards but of course below the waist was a mystery which we had no intention of solving in any circumstance. I suppose in this present day and age that aspect of sexual awareness would be well out of date. In the first year or two at the grammar school my activities outside the schoolroom where mainly concerned with sport. I really enjoyed sport especially football and cricket and on a Saturday afternoon nothing could be better than going with my father to watch Charlton Athletic at their home games. It was with great delight to both of us when in the years before the war Charlton made their way in successive years from the third division into the first. Like all youngsters at that time I felt that every player was a personal friend but of course the greatest one was the celebrated Sam Bartram, the finest goalkeeper at that time.

On a Saturday evening in the summer my greatest enjoyment was to go to Greenwich Pier and watch the paddle steamers returning from the Essex and North Kent Resorts with their cargoes of day trippers. The resorts of Southend, Clacton, Margate and Ramsgate were the destinations of the steamers starting from Tower Bridge. Greenwich was the disembarkation point for those people who lived in south-east London. At the same time they also unloaded the empty crates and bottles which presumably went back to the local breweries and believe me there were a vast quantity of those. I can still remember those paddle steamers coming into sight round the bend in the river where the millennium dome is now situated and as each one was sighted predictions were made as to the name of each steamer. Was it the Royal Eagle or the Royal Sovereign? Or perhaps the Golden Eagle, or even the Crested Eagle. Of course it could have been my mother's favourite, namely the Laguna Belle. Why? Because, as I have mentioned before, it reminded her of her favourite song "Lily of Laguna". I was fascinated by the scores of happy trippers, the noise and bustle as each steamer pulled away to make its way up to the city and make room for the next steamer coming in. I think it will be obvious to all that in my youth I really did have a love for Greenwich. There was the lovely park, the Observatory, the Naval College, the river itself with all its bustle and life and not least the foot tunnel which went from near the pier, under the Thames and came up in a small park on the opposite shore. It was our delight as boys to call to each other from opposite ends of the tunnel so that our voices reverberated off the tiled walls of the tunnel, a prank carried out until the tunnel keeper chased us away. Of course it was awkward if we landed up on the wrong side of the Thames in which case we had to wait until the coast was clear to get back to Greenwich. These were the days before the millennium dome came into existence, before the dry dock for the Cutty Sark was created and certainly before the London Marathon which was established in recent years to start from Blackheath and to run through Greenwich up to the city.

I would like to tell you about my father who in many ways was a source of inspiration to me. Frederick Charles Ransom was born in 1896 and like many others volunteered for service at the beginning of the Great War and he served in France for the whole of the conflict in the Royal Field Artillery. He never talked to me very much about the war but I do know he was devastated when his younger brother, whom I am named after, was killed during the main German offensive in 1918. He was a quiet man, not very outspoken but was very well respected for his views on politics and life in general. He was employed by the Port of London Authority with whom he served until his retirement in 1956 and it is obvious from the commendation he received at that time from Lord Waverley, the chairman of the Authority, that as a senior foreman he was held in high esteem. Most of his work took place in the West India docks which before World War II were the main docks for receiving imports from abroad, including the Commonwealth. My father's main job was to get the ships unloaded in quicktime so that they could get back on the next tide to the far corners of the earth. In this work he had to get the cooperation of the dock workers and their union which of course at times was more than a little difficult, however he seemed to manage this with quite a large slice of diplomacy. I gathered at a later date that he was known to friend and foe as "Artful Arthur." I can only assume that at that time some wag connected my father with the author Arthur Ransome of Swallows and Amazons fame, and the artful bit was an acknowledgement of his ability to get the job done. The memento of service signed by Lord Waverley chairman of the Port of London Authority was also signed by his friends, both colleagues and dock workers. He always voted as a Liberal, and as I felt that he was always right in his thinking, I also voted that way in the many years to come. Although at the present time the party that has inherited those liberal views has got me more than a bit worried! My father died in 1969 at the age of seventy-two from lung cancer. Unfortunately he was a smoker, a habit which came understandably from the Great War and who could deny those men who suffered in the mud and horrors of Flanders the comfort and solace of a cigarette.

I know that many of my generation did not have an easy time during the second world war but personally I feel that people of my father's generation really had the worst deal, for not only did my father suffer the rigours of the trenches in the First World War but later whilst I was away he suffered from the London bombing, and as ships were not getting into the London docks he was called up for fire-fighting and demolition work in the City which as everyone knows was extremely hazardous during the Blitz. My mother also suffered in both world wars in that she worked as a pub landlord in the first (all men having been called up) and was subject to bombing from enemy airships and later on in 1944 she was injured from the blast of a V2 rocket. When I returned home at the end of 1945 I learned from my father that she had been taken into hospital with her body completely blue from the blast and peppered with hundreds of glass splinters from the house windows; however with her London spirit she took pride in showing me the sideboard in the dining room with all its scars. My brother Fred as previously mentioned was just over four years younger than myself and when the Second World War broke out he was still at school, the Addey and Stanhope school having been quickly relocated to the country. I must admit that with the war and in the following years, we went our different ways and I was never going to get very close to my brother. We had different views on life, and I felt on many occasion that he spoilt his future by seeking pastures new and soon finding fault with his lot, the grass was always greener on the other side of the fence.

In 1944 Fred was called up to serve as a signaller in the Devon Regiment and in 1945 married Sheena MacLachlan who was serving in Berlin as a member of the Church Army staff. On their return to England in 1947 they subsequently had two children but were divorced within a year or two. For some reason my brother gave up all his rights to remain in touch with his children, why, I found it hard to understand. Through the years we met up very occasionally and after numerous jobs Fred retired as a postman in the town of Cockermouth. He appeared to have been very fit and active but he died within one month of retirement, and to this day I still feel that I should have made more effort to have kept in touch. Unfortunately the war destroyed many teenage activities, as during the latter part of that time Fred was in Normandy as part of the eighth Army whilst yours truly was still a guest of his Majesty Hirohito of Japan. I am now compiling this book in the year 2013, and the war has been over 68 years, Fred has been dead for 24 years and the regrets are still with me.

I would now take you back to my years at the Addey and Stanhope school which I attended from September 1931 until September 1937. Like any normal schoolboy I enjoyed some subjects of my studies but was less interested in others. However I was always interested in sport and whilst I was at school I very enthusiastically played soccer and cricket though I must admit I did not achieve as high an ability in either as I wished. Normally I played in the second elevens and occasionally got into the first team. I followed national sport in the media avidly following the fortunes of Charlton Athletic in football and Surrey in cricket, and later in life after I left school I continued to play both games up to and after the war. After the war I added the noble game of golf due to the influence of friends north of the border. Of all the games that I played, that final game gave me the greatest pleasure and sense of achievement, although several of those friends referred to were not convinced that my achievement in the game had reached the heights expected north of the Border. My six years at the secondary school can be divided into two parts, the first up to the summer of 1935 and the second from then until I left school in September 1937.

In 1935 my parents like many in similar circumstances took advantage of a substantial housing boom at that time and we moved to a new estate at Eltham which had been built just off the main road from Eltham to Woolwich. Apart from being a modern house with up-to-date facilities it enabled my father to reach the main docks more easily; a slight drawback was the further distance to travel to the school at New Cross. By 1935 I suppose I was a more assured teenager and I enjoyed the new environment which led me to explore the countryside of Kent. Like all other lads of my age I was now taking an interest in girls and since I was at a co-educational school one could say the talent was there to look at! The girl that sent my senses reeling was pretty, brunette, had long hair and her name was Margaret Clarke. Why is it at the age of ninety-three you can still remember the first girl that stirred your passions? Mark you my efforts to pursue my amorous intentions were hardly successful, my achievements mainly consisted of walking her home on the odd occasion. That trip involved walking from New Cross out past New Cross Gate and a fair way down the Old Kent Road which meant I ended up further away from home and consequently arriving in Eltham to be greeted by questions as to why I was late home which of course with youthful indifference I ignored. On one memorable occasion I extracted a promise from Margaret that we would meet up to go to the Odeon cinema in the Old Kent Road one Friday evening; yes you've guessed it, she stood me up and after standing in the rain for about an hour I returned home bedraggled and not a happy lad. The following Monday at school Margaret greeted me with a smile, we had a cheery chat and my wrath went out the window. Later in life I am happy to say I was a little more successful with women but my failure with Margaret still haunts me. We both left school in 1937 and went our separate ways but met just one more time at the end of the war at a school reunion when I turned up in uniform and Margaret turned up with two children. Ah well c'est la vie or whatever!!

Towards the end of my school career I went on a couple of school trips or journeys to the continent and these normally took place in the spring when of course accommodation could be found more easily for parties of about 50 including four or five teachers. The trip I remember most vividly was to Malmedy in Belgium. Whilst the main party were ensconced in the main hotel in the town square, four or five of us had to be accommodated in a local cafe and it was with great delight that a few mates and myself drew the lucky straws. I still fondly remember the Café Laroche, the proprietor and his wife and of course their son who taught us quite a bit about life, including the ability to play table tennis. As teenagers we of course promised to abide with a curfew hour of nine o'clock but the atmosphere of a vibrant continental cafe in the evening proved too much and I'm sorry to say, the promise was broken. It was one of the happiest times in my youth I can remember after the war I was shocked and upset that eight years after our trip Malmedy was subject to violation and atrocities at the hands of the Germans during the Battle of the Bulge. I rather suspect that the Café Laroche is no more but I do hope the family survived to enjoy freedom and the rest of their lives. Also during that trip to Belgium we made a journey to Cologne for a day, my recollection of the city at that time was that it was bustling, prosperous with many flags flying including of course those with swastikas. Little did I realise that in three years time I would be sitting in the canteen at Woolwich barracks listening to Neville Chamberlain's declaration of war against Germany. It was a time when events were moving fast and the years of my youth were flying by, but of course I was just one of many.

In my last year or two at the grammar school and for a couple of years afterwards I took up an interest in athletics. I started off doing quite well in school events mainly in the short sprints up to 440 yards. Later on I was more successful at the longer distances even cross country events so much so that I joined Herne Hill athletics club for training purposes. Again this interest was curtailed and in fact abandoned by the outbreak of the Second World War. After leaving school I dropped running competitively but I still went to running tracks to build up my stamina and strengthen my legs, an asset I was to be thankful for later in the war. One of the tracks I think was at Charlton Park and I can remember seeing a small man who wore glasses also training there. He seemed to reel off circuit after circuit during his training without showing any signs of fatigue, in fact no one could keep up with him and it was only later that I discovered he was Sydney Wooderson.

Sydney Wooderson in the years before the war was one of Britain's greatest middle-distance runners and probably prior to the war his greatest achievement was to hold the world mile record at 4 min six seconds. If he had been able to continue his training and preparation without the war intervening he might have been the first man to beat the time of 4 min for the mile. His poor eyesight prevented him from doing active service but I learned afterwards that he had served in the Royal Pioneer Corps and also in the R.E.M.E. After the war I believe he was a member of the 1948 Olympic team without success and although everyone thought he should carry the Olympic torch into Wembley Stadium it was overruled because of his slightly build, wore glasses and so was not considered imposing enough. His career was and is of interest to me as like myself he was born in Camberwell and it is a coincidence that he died just before Christmas in 2006 at the age of ninety-two, the age I reached last year.

I had now reached the age of seventeen and would be leaving the Addey and Stanhope school at the end of the 1937 summer term. In those days teenagers were pretty innocent, at least I was and it follows that I viewed the years to come with some trepidation. I cannot recall that I had a definite ambition, one of my best subjects at school was art but it was unlikely I would get much support in being an artist. In those days grammar school boys were advised by all and sundry to pursue banking or insurance as a livelihood, since employment in these areas were considered safe, carried a reasonable salary and what was even more important at the end of the day was pensionable. Little did I know what lay in store for me, how at that time could I visualise a lifetime stretching from 1937 until 2013. Maybe I should have been a little worried!

# The Pre-war Years

## 1937–1939: Working in London until War

The beginning of 1937 involved taking the University of London's examinations and I obtained their certificate with credits in my favourite subjects, namely mathematics, geography and art. As I only obtained a pass in English I did not reach matriculation standard which would have enabled me to get into most major businesses without a great deal of bother and pave the way into a university. The headmaster felt I should stay on and resit the English paper but circumstances at home did not make this possible, so in the late summer of 1937 I began the process of looking for a job at the age of seventeen, completely unaware of what lay before me. There was in existence at that time a secondary schools headmaster's association which had connections with many business companies and if you registered with them they would help you to find a vacancy. In addition you made your own enquiries to banks and insurance companies as it was considered in those times that getting a position in that type of company would lead you to a job for life and a pension at the end of service. The major banks tended to be the target of grammar school boys who had elected to leave school rather than continue to university. I did seek more than one interview with banks but despite having a top class pass in mathematics it was to no avail. In fact on presenting myself to the head office of Lloyds bank near the Mansion House I got no further than the first question, namely "Does your father have an account with us?" which ruled me out immediately. Possibly in today's climate that action would be classified as discrimination but in those days I suppose it was a case of dog eat dog.

However I did get an invitation to go for an interview with an Australian assurance company, and on turning up at their United Kingdom head office at the east end of Cheapside in London, I was horrified to find myself one of 10 applicants. I thought I made a reasonable impression but a regret letter duly arrived together with another letter inviting me to an interview with a Japanese company called Mitsui Bussan Kaisha. If I remember rightly the offices of this company were in Leadenhall Street and I duly turned up there on the Monday morning a week after being turned down by the Australian company. The main office was a very long room with very large desks spaced out along each side and at each desk sat a Japanese and an European face-to-face. I was taken to a small anteroom lined with shelves holding very large industrial books and several teleprinter machines. This was my first meeting with the Japanese and little did I realise it was an omen leading to a relationship which would occur in about four years time. My job as a junior was to decode messages and take them to the appropriate desks and it soon became obvious to me that each desk dealt either with a special commodity or a trade route. I learned later in life that at that time the company had a fleet of about 40 merchant or tramp steamers operating all over the world and that the two men at each desk were arranging for the shipment of goods from port to port in the quickest and cheapest way. It soon became obvious to me that there would be no slacking in this job and that any wage earned would be well deserved but at the end of my first week I was able to say goodbye to the Japanese for the time. On the Friday of that week I received a letter from the Australian assurance company offering me their vacancy as apparently the first choice had gone to a bank and I was second reserve. Thankfully I accepted, sent a letter of resignation to the Japanese who responded without comment with a postal order for one pound, thirteen shillings and four pence. I don't think the Japanese were very pleased but they were probably less so during the war which followed when two thirds of their fleet were sunk by the activities of Allied submarines and aircraft.

The following week I turned up at the head office of the National Mutual of Australasia to work as an assurance clerk and was with them until the outbreak of the Second World War which proved to be almost a period of two years. In 1937 the offices of the company were in a modern building in the area behind St Paul's cathedral, looking directly down Cheapside towards the Bank. Journeying each day from home in Eltham required me to use the southern electric train from Eltham Park station to Cannon Street station in the city, the journey taking about 30 minutes and during the two years I hardly ever got a seat, the train almost on every occasion being packed almost to suffocation. A brisk walk followed up from the station through St Mary le Bow churchyard and along the western part of Cheapside to arrive at the office by 9 a.m. The manager or secretary was Adam Currie and after a brief interview I was placed as a junior clerk (on probation) in the accounts department at a commencing salary of £60 per annum on the understanding that if my work gave satisfaction that amount would be raised each year by a further £20 per annum. I cannot remember where it came from but I also got the impression that marriage was frowned upon until you had reached a salary of about £400 per annum. Following this piece of knowledge I made the rapid calculation that I would probably be getting married when I reached the age of thirty-seven, but fortunately I made that status when I was twenty-six, much to my relief. However there was much to be thankful for; it was a pleasant office, kindly colleagues and the important prospect of retirement with a pension. What more could a man ask for? I soon made friends, in particular with Howard Agar and George Young who had joined the company a year or two before me.

After 1939 I still kept in touch with Howard and his charming Irish wife Meta but sadly I recently received news that Meta had died and Howard was now in a nursing home. George Young lived with his parents in Eltham and our paths in life continued to cross during the war and afterwards but that story comes later. My work in the accounts department (under the supervision of Howard) tended to be a little boring but at times, especially at the end of each month it became extremely hectic. At this time branches throughout the UK sent in their monthly accounts which had to be totted up and balanced with the help of an ancient manual adding machine, a task normally carried out, owing to the racket in made, away from the department and left me sweating and with an aching arm. I know that I probably did other jobs but that one at the end of the month still remains in my memory. The day ended at 5.30 p.m. followed by a rush with all the other thousands of commuters down to Cannon Street station to be packed in like sardines into the first available train; we also worked on a Saturday until 12.30 p.m. and an additional chore for us as juniors was to help after normal hours in despatching post. The turn to do this last duty came round about one week in three and in addition there was extra work at the end of each month to get the accounts balanced which meant working for extra hours in the evening. Needless to say all this extra overtime was unpaid but in those day accepted in good grace; mark you how times have changed! We were allowed one hour for lunch and as departments were not allowed to be un-manned we as juniors more or less were told when we could go for lunch. Round about mid day Howard, George and I made a beeline for the Joe Lyons restaurant across the road from the office where using the self service facility we each loaded up our trays with a pie, chips and a cup of tea for the princely sum of about one shilling, a meal which we repeated daily almost without change for two years.

One of our activities outside the office involved playing cricket, an office team was organised and during the summer months we played a number of friendly matches. In nearly all our matches we were well beaten but our opponents always seemed keen to play us. I can only believe that being an Australian company there was a desire to play and beat us, this vindictiveness in cricket between Australia and England existed during the war as I well know it still does, quite rightly. I distinctly remember a match against a firm of bookmakers where we were skittled out for about 20 runs and lost by 10 wickets, a match in which I opened the innings, scored five runs and saw 10 wickets fall at the other end, not exactly a jaw dropping feat. But so what, in the bar later all scores are forgotten over a pint or two. My only worry on these occasions was the fact that I had very little money in my pocket as I often only started the weekend with about half a crown to my name. From the princely sum of five pounds per month which I received as salary there were deductions. My season ticket on the train amounting to £1.13.4d, approximately 21 pie and chips amounting to £1.1.0.d, the cost of my clothes, toiletries and incidentals, and not forgetting a deduction for the employee's pension contribution. I had no car, cricket matches in Surrey incurred travel expenditure so when on one occasion I was delegated to escort a young lady member, who was to act as scorer to the match, I was extremely embarrassed to ask her to pay her own fare, but luckily I was able to stand her a drink later on even though it was a half pint of shandy. As George and I both lived fairly close to each other, just before the war we joined a local cricket club called the Beachcombers whose president was a gentleman who wrote an article in the Daily Express under that name. Needless to say neither of us made much of an impact in that team.

The front windows of the office looked directly down Cheapside towards the Bank and it was a great viewpoint from which to watch processions making their way round St Paul's down Cheapside to the Guildhall. These processions were in honour of a famous person or persons being taken to the Guildhall for a lunch given by the Lord Mayor of London. Whenever these occurred we would rush to the window as they normally involved a number of splendid open carriages escorted by a squadron of lifeguards. The one I really remember was in I think 1938 when King Carol of Romania was welcomed and it was the one occasion when the King's apparel outshone that of the lifeguards. He was dressed in full uniform plus a silver breastplate, silver helmet with spike and plume; he looked glorious and in addition he was accompanied by Madam Lupescu wearing a startling silver gown complete with furs and feather headdress. As far as I can remember

Madam Lupescu was the Kings third wife, the first two marriages having been annulled and I think that she was the centre of court gossip all over Europe. At any rate the whole procession was a bobby dazzler as you might say.

1938 went by and as we entered the New Year it became apparent that the clouds of war were darkening over Europe and in early spring the British government made a strong effort to bolster up the Territorial Army and a number of recruiting booths were set up in the area outside the Mansion House. George Young and I were blithely waiting for the approach of midday and the prospect of our pie and chips when the manager Adam Currie appeared and engaged us in an unexpected friendly conversation. He enquired whether we had thoughts of joining the Terriers adding at the same time that the company, if we joined, would add an extra week of holiday to help us to participate in the Terriers autumn camp. The extra holiday week proved irresistible so the next day at lunchtime George and I trotted down to the Mansion House to sign up, thus ensuring that in the future we would meet several members of the Japanese nation. It's true that you should never volunteer, I did, and I also ignored the omen that surfaced in my first job, so not only did I suffer the consequences but I took poor old George with me. The recruiting stalls were manned by various branches of his Majesty's forces but George and I having already decided that we would like to join a unit close to our homes settled on the 65th Regiment of the Royal Artillery whose headquarters were close by at Lee Green. I was quite happy with this decision as my father had served in the First World War in the Royal Artillery. Round about that time Howard who lived in Acton over the other side of London had joined the Royal Engineers. George and I attended weekly training sessions at the drill hall at Lee Green along with a crowd of other lads. Apparently the enthusiasm of British youth to be ready for war that might be coming had meant that the regiments already in existence soon filled up, and like many others we were drafted into what were initially called second line regiments, ours was subsequently numbered 118.

The news relating to happenings in Europe was getting worse so training was stepped up but this was hampered by the lack of equipment although items, mainly clothing etc were issued. The instructors were mainly from the regular Army and believe me they kept us on our toes with the basic square bashing and comments as to our appearance and ability. These comments were never complimentary, in addition on one notable occasion George upset the regimental sergeant major. George's father was a high-ranking police officer at Scotland Yard and drove a beautiful Armstrong Sidley car which on this occasion George decided to borrow for the evenings drill session. George picked me up and we drove down in style to the drill hall and parked in the one remaining space, which proved later on, as explained rather forcibly by the Sgt major, to belong to the commanding officer. In the stream of words directed at us we only recognised "MOVE IT", the other words we came to recognise in the years to follow. Amongst the clothing that was issued was a tin helmet and a pair of boots which were not to be used but to be kept for the fortnight's training camp which we were told would occur in the early summer, in the beautiful holiday spot of Dartmoor. It would have been better if we had been told to use them on every occasion, even going to work, as we would have been spared the agony of blistered feet tramping over the moors later on.

George and I were informed after time that we were to be trained as surveyors who we gathered were responsible for pointing the guns in the right direction and hitting, hopefully the right target. The training fortnight duly arrived and the Regiment set off in a special train for Okehampton in Devon, the journey taking what seemed like a week in carriages lacking toilet facilities. Once arriving we marched in pouring rain up to the camp to find that our accommodation consisted of three sided horse stables, the open side faced the elements, as of course as everyone knows horses do not like to face the wind. Guns and equipment were kept at the camp and in the following fortnight in which the weather never abated, we were trained in their use from daybreak to about 6 p.m. Providing all the equipment had been cleaned of mud and polished to the sergeant major's satisfaction we were then allowed to crawl into our stable, get under our damp blanket and on to our damp straw mattress. The army food at the camp was horrible although later in my life I would have accepted it with delight but on one or two occasions we were allowed to make our weary way to the canteen in the evening and purchase egg and chips for the sum of one shilling and sixpence. Bearing in mind the amount of our pay at work we had not come with "holiday spending money", therefore the Army pay of one shilling a day did little to cheer us up. After the fortnight we made our way back to Okehampton station in the mud and rain and returned very happily to our homes in the warmth and sunshine of London. I was quite surprised when I turned up at the drill hall on our next training night to find that I had been promoted to the rank of unpaid acting lance bombardier, this dubious promotion did not mean very much except I could give orders if I so wished to the gunners, as privates are known in the

Royal artillery. As at this time we were more or less all pals together, all orders I tended to give were received with a little bit of mickey taking, specially by George, in whom I was most disappointed! At this time although the news from Europe was looking pretty grim I don't think we realised how close the outbreak of war was and that soon we would be soldiers carrying out orders in earnest. To us the Prime Minister Neville Chamberlain seemed to be running about like a headless chicken achieving nothing, and sure enough in the week prior to the declaration of war, the Territorial Army was mobilised.

# War Years in the United Kingdom

## 1939–1941

We received our papers to report to the drill hall on 1st September 1939 that day being a Friday and in full kit we were marched to the main artillery barracks at Woolwich. On the Sunday morning of 3rd September we were seated in the canteen listening to the radio and we heard Neville Chamberlain at 11 o'clock declare war on Germany. I think we marked the occasion with a bun and a mug of tea but we were unhappy to learn later that we were confined to barracks until further notice and that all outside contact of any kind was forbidden. A few weeks later restrictions were eased a little but leaving the barracks overnight would require a pass which was seldom forthcoming and of course mail was censored. I learned later that my parents were under the impression that the Regiment had immediately been sent to France. This in a way was quite amusing as looking from the barrack room to the South East, across Woolwich Common, my parent's house on Shooters Hill could be clearly seen at a distance of 1 mile, what I needed was some sort of signalling apparatus or even a pigeon! For the first month or two we were billeted in the old dormitory type blocks which were to the rear of the main long building which faced on to a parade ground and these dormitories had ground and first floor accommodation and faced each other across a small parade ground. Observing the age and the furnishings in the dormitories there is no doubt that they had witnessed the departure in days gone by other unfortunates such as ourselves to the far corners of the Empire to participate in jolly jaunts such as "Waterloo" and "the Relief of Khartoum". There followed a soul destroying cycle of drills, weapon training and on one momentous occasion inoculation against every conceivable disease. The parade on which we received our jabs proved to be very amusing and I would say was to the detriment of Army morale, in that on the sight of hypodermic needles being waved in front of them one or two of the lads immediately fainted, and as the injections proceeded the number hitting the ground increased. It was obvious from his language, the sergeant major was not pleased; it became a case of pick up the casualties, throw them on their beds, and to report back as soon as possible for an hour's physical training in order to get whatever had been injected moving through their bodies.

Never-ending sessions of drills took place on the small parade ground as the sergeant major made it quite clear that before we would be allowed to drill on the main parade ground, in front of the facade of the barracks, we would have to achieve drill efficiency of Brigade of guards' standard. He had no intention of parading a rabble such as us in front of the windows of the officer's mess, it could have easily put them off their appetites. Later on bearing in mind I had already learned my lesson regarding volunteering, when the sergeant major on one occasion asked if anyone was good at athletics I said yes, what a fool! I found myself playing for the Royal Artillery against the Irish Guards in a rugby union game! I had never played the game in my life and although I made this point to the sergeant major he dismissed my objections and simply informed me that I would be playing as a three-quarter and that on receiving the ball I was to run like hell! I was lucky, the game ended in a three points each draw and I successfully avoided any of the 6ft, 14 stone opponents. Passes out of barracks were pretty impossible but I remember that on one occasion George's father drove up to the main gate in a Scotland Yard squad car complete with chauffeur and demanded to see me and George. The Sentry faced with this show of authority was not prepared to prevent George and me going off for afternoon tea at home, we of course were dropped back in style for evening roll call.

Later on we were moved as a unit out of the main barracks and moved to the old horse artillery buildings called Shrapnel barracks on the other side of Woolwich Common. Accommodation was in dormitories on the first floor as the ground floor was still laid out to accommodate horses. By now I was a member of E troop, 260 battery as a paid lance bombardier with a duty to rouse the gunners in the morning. This of course required me to get up well before 6 a.m. and armed with my cane I took great delight in marching through the dormitory rattling the beds and if necessary whacking an occupant. I think I may have got above myself but I was soon physically brought to earth as on one dark winter morning some b****r left a trap door open and I dropped about 12 feet onto the stone floor of the horses stables, luckily the horses were long gone! I had sore ankles for a month! As a lance bombardier I was occasionally given charge of a small guard of three men and one duty which occurred was to guard German prisoners at nearby Brook Hospital. We were not allowed to talk to them but I believe they were injured survivors of

German planes which had been shot down in the early days of the war.

About this time we also started receiving vehicles and some artillery pieces; the vehicles including motor cycles were in the main from civilian sources and were treated with Army paint to make them look respectable. I think that the artillery pieces came from a number of sources including museums as I remember that one 4.5 howitzer had been labelled "for drill purposes only". I often wondered what would have happened if it had been loaded and fired, I didn't fancy being near it on such an occasion! At this time very little was happening on the continent of Europe, the period was designated in the press as the "phoney war" and at Woolwich I can only remember two incidents during that period which broke the monotony. The first involved about 200 personnel manning about half a dozen open lorries with everyone dressed in full kit including steel helmets and rifles, the procession thus formed was driven out of one gate, entered another 20 yards away and then out again through the first gate. This manoeuvre was performed several times and with cameras present we were told to cheer and look happy. I believe all this was for propaganda purposes but I can't remember ever seeing the film! The second occurred when our battery was sent for a few days down to Margate on the Kent coast, a manoeuvre completed with difficulty owing to the poor state of our civilian vehicles. I can only think that this was done to cheer up the citizens of that area and I had my doubts about that. However on this occasion I was in charge of a small guard of three men with a couple of 18 pounders which had their muzzles pointed in through the Esplanade rails, when a Rolls-Royce pulled up carrying a chauffeur and a well-dressed old lady. I was beckoned to the car and presented with a £10 note (unfamiliar at the time to me) as a token of her belief that the safety of the country was in our good hands. Unfortunately the gift was observed by the three men of the guard who suggested or rather demanded the money be split, however as the car departed I lined them up and ordered a royal salute for the dear old lady!

In the early spring the regiment was ordered to the south coast and I think that in the main we were happy about this as life at Woolwich had become rather monotonous. Our battery found themselves in Eastbourne and as a group of surveyors we were billeted in a boarding house on the seafront and I regret to say that as a group of youngsters in early 1940 we were not well behaved. The landlady had a lot to put up with, beds were broken during skylarking and there was a lot of noise sometimes into the early hours of the morning. During the day we were at the drill hall down by the harbour for training and lectures, returning to the billet after five o'clock. In a way it was like returning to school and it was a great improvement on the regimental life at Woolwich; we even became honorary members of the Eastbourne Winkle Club, the dubious benefits of which I have forgotten. Later on the battery was moved into the vacant catholic girls' school and to our amusement each soldier was given a cubicle, which was a change from the usual dormitory. The only trouble was space, as each man tended to be larger than a small schoolgirl, requiring his feet to stick out of the door. There is no doubt that the catholic girls' school in all its life had never heard such language when at night the gunners attempted to find their own cubicle after lights out! Outdoor activities then increased, the battery began to dig gunpits on Beachy Head and the four pieces of ordnance we had, were installed. At this time I was designated to be an observation post assistant and the observation post officer would be second lieutenant Mr Robinson who was placed in charge of E troop. My association with Mr Robinson was to last for about a year and involved a number of humorous incidents mainly due to the fact that for an observation officer he had poor sight (it was rumoured that in civilian life he had been a prison warder). He was not prepared to rectify this with spectacles, as he felt that it detracted from his very smart appearance as an officer. I think that by now you may have come to the conclusion that the early days of the war resembled incidents as depicted in that well-known BBC series Dad's Army, and in doing so you would not be very far wrong! One of the observation posts turned out to be Pevensey Castle, and I remember being given a rather inappropriate Yale key to open the wooden gate into the ruined Norman castle. As I stood on the crumbling battlements and looked out to sea it came to me that I was at the spot where William the Conqueror had come ashore in 1066 and there was I, Lance Bombardier Ransom keeping an eye out for the Germans who might conceivably decide to choose the same spot in Pevensey Bay to land. By God I hope not!

By now we had reached the beginning of May and it had appeared that matters were "hotting up" on the continent and that things were not looking too good, so much so that the French army quickly disintegrated in front of the German blitzkrieg. The retreat of the British army followed and what is now history, the evacuation of the major part of it took place between 26 May and 4 June. As far as we were concerned we were placed under a red alert and as far as I can remember our orders were from our high positions on Beachy Head to target the shore and in particular Eastbourne Pier, and await the possibility of the enemy following up the evacuation. There was of course the chance that units from Dunkirk would make their way back our way and in any case with the antiquated guns we had I doubted if we could have hit Eastbourne let alone the pier. We all know Hitler did not instruct his generals to pursue our forces and carry out an invasion, and as we were all aware at the time as to the strength of our defences on our part of the south coast, I feel we had a large slice of good luck. In fact I feel that the War Office must have come to the same conclusion, namely that the defences on the south coast had to be improved, so we were moved out of the area to East Anglia, presumably they had other units available who were better equipped and possibly better trained. Thus our nondescript convoy of vehicles and guns made its way northwards via London to Norfolk, a journey one would have thought could have been made in a day but coupled with breakdowns and the opportunity taken by some to visit their homes in south-east London, vehicles were still arriving at our first destination near Norwich three days later!

The policy of the army chiefs at that time seemed to be enshrined in the belief that it was good for units not to be settled down but to be moved often; maybe they had the welfare of local populations at heart! And so in the latter half of 1940 we occupied locations in Norfolk. The two that I remember with fondness were at Swanton Morley and Weybourne on the coast. Whilst moving to these coastal areas the battery encamped for a night or two north of Norwich giving rise to the saga known to us as "the battle of Holt". This was a time when rumour raised the possibility of Germans landing on the Norfolk coast. Accordingly Jack Chalker (signaller) and I were positioned in an observation post on a bend two miles north of Holt when to our dismay we heard the sound of rifle fire at our rear. This was rather disconcerting since any Germans should be in front of us! However after a fitful night an explanation was forthcoming. Apparently the extensive rifle fire had been caused by two sentries, one Welsh and the other Irish. The Welshman posted on one side of the vehicle park had challenged a piece of glowing fungus and getting no answer fired off a few shots, whereupon the Irishman on the other side of the park on receiving some bullets past his ears returned fire in good measure. There is no doubt that people from the provinces do tend to get excitable at times! I perhaps should mention at this point that I had more or less lost touch with George Young as the initial batch of surveyors had been split up and distributed among the troops of each battery, with the two batteries being increased in number to three with George joining the third battery. Weybourne was a delightful place and the antiquated guns of the troop were dug in behind the beach with the rest of the troop ensconced in the sand dunes in front. Mr Robinson had now been promoted to full lieutenant and had been joined by second Lt Samuel Hall whose responsibility was the ordnance. It may not be known that to have the name Samuel Hall in the Army was not an advantage as the Royal artillery album of marching songs and ditties contained one which made a direct reference to that individual who went through life lacking one of two bodily appendages!

In front of us in the sand dunes was an anti-tank unit who in the main kept themselves to themselves, and were very quiet, except from time to time a Scottish voice would call "Sgt McGregor tae the phone" which was answered back by another Scottish voice "Sgt McGregor is a wae oot." I cannot remember any other conversation from this unit and it was repeated quite a number of times during the day, giving rise to speculation amongst us as to where Sgt McGregor spent his time! There were times when we anticipated the call and replied in our cockney voices to the effect that dear old Sgt McGregor had buggered off! Our idyllic life at Weybourne after a few weeks was upset by Lt Robinson receiving the news that in the near future we would receive a top brass inspection. We were going to be allowed to fire off one or two rounds at corrugated iron targets set up on the beach, accordingly Lt Robinson made sure that the gun crews were both smart in appearance and efficient in gun drill. Inspection day duly came with the arrival of high ranked officers complete with red tabs and shooting sticks and I can only sum up the day with two army words, together they both signified that all had not gone too well, in other words there had been a f*** up. The day ended with a brigadier tapping Lieutenant Robinson on the shoulder and promising he would return in a month and unless there was an improvement, the two pips on his shoulder would be reduced to one. A high degree of activity then ensued; distances to targets were measured to the inch and angles minutely measured. In addition, Robinson felt that a little ingenuity was called for, accordingly an old fisherman's hut high up on the beach was commandeered and an 18 pounder placed in it, to be manned by its crew on the great day. When that arrived everything went off splendidly, the brass hats were duly impressed with the accuracy of the guns, although it must be said the throwing open of the fisherman's hut doors and the firing of a blank round from therein was spectacular rather than convincing. When the gun was fired the whitewash on the walls of the hut disintegrated, and bearing in mind that whitewash had been coated on year after year since Queen Victoria's coronation, the white cloud that emerged lasted, it seemed, for about 15 minutes. This would probably have been enough time for a German Panzer division to make its way up the beach since the gun team, looking like an advert for self raising flour, would not have seen them coming. However Lieutenant Robinson's ingenuity was rewarded and some weeks later he was made a captain which was celebrated in due manner by all and sundry at the local pub.

Regarding Robinson's promotion I should have mentioned that earlier on in the battery's wanderings he commissioned his portrait to be painted, this having been done by Jack Chalker a signaller who happened to be a very proficient artist and in this portrait Captain Robinson had been depicted of course as a lieutenant. So when the battery again moved, E Troop occupied the lovely village of Swanton Morley and there the captain recalled the picture from his home in London, and ordered Jack to add the extra pip to each shoulder of his splendid uniform. In Jack's eyes and as a dedicated artist this was sacrilege, however orders is orders! The guns were positioned a mile or two from the village but I as an observer and Jack Chalker as my signaller were put in the tower of Swanton Morley church whilst the captain and second lieutenant Samuel Hall were billeted in the village pub namely the Papermakers Arms. Jack and I moved out kit up to the Bell room halfway up the church tower and in a time of emergency we were to move up to the roof with our equipment, and be prepared, with the addition of Capt Robinson to bring fire down if necessary on the RAF aerodrome which lay about two miles away. The aerodrome at that time was home to heavy bombers which were beginning to make sorties into Europe and when they took off laden with bombs and fuel it seemed to Jack and I that they only missed the top of the church tower (and us) by about a couple of feet. At that time the Royal Air Force Regiment had not come into existence so defence of aerodromes fell to units like ourselves. In fact as there was a possibility still of enemy paratroopers landing on aerodromes, in a last resort we were prepared to shell the aerodrome at Swanton Morley even if there were RAF personnel still occupying the field.

Jack and I enjoyed our home in the bell tower but whenever we had a few shillings in our pockets we would go across to the pub for a drink where captain Robinson was keeping himself refreshed without cost. This our dear Captain achieved by playing poor lieutenant Hall at snooker, how could Sammy refuse a challenge to a game, made by a superior officer? Before long Capt Robinson's wife joined him in the Papermakers Arms and as a very attractive woman her appearance was appreciated by the rank and file, especially as on a warm day she tended to ride through the village on her bicycle dressed in a skimpy silk dress which tended to float up in the wind. However turning to more military matters it was about this time that we lost our antiquated guns and acquired a set of 75 mm guns which apparently had been stored in America since 1918, they were brand new, having been manufactured too late to have been used in the First World War. These guns had large iron rimmed wheels and could only be towed at about 10 m.p.h. but a solution was found by hauling them up by ramps into the bodies of 30 hundredweight trucks fitted with winches. The ammunition also came with them, the shells weighing about 12lbs each but on the one occasion when we tried the guns out on a small range in

Norfolk about 50% of the shells failed to explode, in addition they were very hazardous to handle. Luckily in time to come, they were the replaced by brand new British 25 pounders complete with up-to-date gun towers.

We eventually left the delights of Norfolk, especially sad to say goodbye to Swanton Morley whose villagers had been extremely kind to us, but 1940 was beginning to draw to a close and 118 Field Regiment was beginning to take training and efficiency more seriously. The division made its way into the Midlands and for a while we were located in the area around Stourbridge and Wolverhampton and while we were there our artillery unit made a visit to the Welsh training camp at Trawsfynydd in the Mount Snowdon area. As far as I can recollect this was a wet, muddy and miserable excursion and I regret to say not much of a welcome from the Welsh in that area. I learned later that this area was noted for its Welsh nationalism and following the end of the war further training in the area was opposed by Plaid Cymru who at that time were against military conscription. I believe at that time we were still using the 75 mm guns so it's possible we left behind a considerable number of unexploded shells! We were quite happy to return to the Midlands where at one stage we had a pleasant time billeted in Shugborough Hall, the seat of the earls of Lichfield. If my memory serves me right it was at this time that we received all our modern equipment, sparkling brand-new, but destined at some future date to be hardly used and lost. Eventually at the end of 1940 we made our way northwards via the army camp at Catterick to Scotland. As the whole division was to be located in the Scottish Borders steps were taken to send advance parties from every unit to recce areas for occupation and billeting and it became my lot to be included in the team being sent on behalf of our battery. Accordingly one officer, Lt Thwaites, myself, now a full bombardier and six men set off in two 15 hundredweight trucks for what we considered was a foreign land. We left off in the early morning and as soon as we crossed the Scottish border we ran into snow which became deeper as we journeyed on. It was early December and soon it was pitch dark, being wartime there were no indications as to where we were, how far we had gone and how far we had to go. About 6 p.m. we reached a small town and as we slowly drove down the main street I spotted one individual, head down against the snow, trudging along the pavement. Calling out in my distinct London accent I enquired as to our whereabouts and received a grudgingly reply which sounded like" Oick" which I considered to be a little unkind and so drove on without thanking the person. It was only at a later date that I learned I had misjudged the native in that the reply given was the local pronunciation of the name of Hawick, quite a substantial town in the Borders. Later that night we arrived at the small village of Walkerburn to meet up with other advance parties representing the other battery, and the headquarters personnel, following which a decision was taken as to the allocation of areas.. The regimental headquarters unit would remain in Walkerburn, one battery would go a further two or three miles to Innerleithen and the other an extra seven miles to Peebles. The decision as to who would go the furthest with conditions being terrible and snow a foot deep, was decided by tossing a coin, needless to say our lieutenant lost the toss. So, on we made our weary way reaching Peebles about 10 o'clock at night pulling up outside what was then the old Priory and today in 2013 is the main post office. Lieutenant Thwaites indicated that myself and the six gunners were to make the best of things by bedding down in the dilapidated and deserted Priory and after receiving the customary salute he set off for the comfort of the Tontine hotel further down the High Street (bless you Jack I'm all right). We bedded down to the best of our ability on the wooden floors, in the light from oil lamps, and were soon fast asleep but awoke before dawn soaking wet with water running across the floor. The water coming from a burst pipe was prevented from causing further discomfort by cutting the pipe with a blow from an army axe and turning the end of the pipe out of the window. We learned that the Polish Army had preceded us in the town and looking around the walls of the Priory we were in admiration of the graffiti they had left behind, we couldn't understand the language but the murals were quite specific! That morning we brewed ourselves tea and ate our emergency rations, following which I made arrangements with a local plumber for the mending of the water pipe. In view of the lake that had now formed outside the Priory I got the impression that the Scottish artisan did not have a good opinion of the English, mark you I may have been mistaken, I could not understand a word he said. Having got things tidied up to the best of my ability and Mr Thwaites had yet to make an appearance (probably coping with a full Scottish breakfast) I sauntered across the road to the paper shop and there within 24-hours of being in Scotland for the first time, I met my future wife.

The charming brunette across the counter greeted me with a smile which in a way unnerved me, but pulling myself together, I asked if the News Chronicle was available and to my astonishment it was, and naturally the trip across to the paper shop became of course a regular excursion. The Polish Army had departed for pastures new but most of the billeting arrangements were still there in the form of church halls and other accommodation; there was also in existence the old bullring which could house the guns, the limbers and the gun towers. The local stream, the Eddlestone water which ran into the Tweed also had a ford in which equipment could be cleaned so the battery was soon able to make itself at home and be ready for manoeuvres and training in the border area. My trips to the paper shop continued and if on occasion I was unable to make it Helen saved my paper for me. In addition there was the added bonus that I was able to meet her some evenings at the Church of Scotland canteen for service men, where she was on occasion a volunteer helper. It was a hard winter with plenty of snow and the manoeuvres amongst the border hills was very tiring with guns and vehicles at times been stuck in mud, snow, and in openings in stone dykes and on return to Peebles all equipment of course had to be cleaned and polished; they were long days. After a month or two of this we were convinced that our eventual destination was probably Norway or maybe Iceland, how wrong we were! In the meantime my pursuit of Helen was proceeding quite nicely, in addition to the paper shop and canteen we met on occasion for a walk in the local Hay Lodge Park and eventually I was invited to meet her father and mother. Later I had no difficulty whatsoever in coping with the Scottish dialect whether it came from the Highlands, the Lothians, and the Borders or even from Glasgow! But in the winter of 1940/41 it was an effort to understand, although I coped with Helen's soft Border accent without difficulty. In due course I met Helen's parents and was treated to an excellent tea, and I was received with smiles. Mrs Crawford was charming and her husband also, if a little dour.

Sad to say I didn't understand a word either of them uttered (although surely my south London cockney English would have been perfectly clear to them?). I thanked them for their hospitality and returned to the Priory determined to brush up on the language difficulty. After time the winter snow disappeared and we were more able to appreciate the beautiful countryside around Peebles with the River Tweed running through the town, which itself had about 6000 inhabitants. The locals made us very welcome and we were able to appreciate the shops, the tearooms and the bakeries, not forgetting the pubs and hotels. There seemed to be, with regard to the latter, a rule preventing females from visiting bars and another forbidding all serving of alcohol on a Sunday. However we found it very enjoyable in Peebles and as you might say when in Rome do as the Romans do". I certainly had no cause for complaint, between the manoeuvres both military and in my courting Jack was a happy lad. I would have been delighted to have seen out the war in Peebles but of course in time it came to an end and in the second week of April 1941 we were on the move again down to the Midlands. So it was with tears that I said goodbye to my Scottish girlfriend, vowing that I would never forget her and at the first opportunity I would return; how could I forget Helen Anderson Crawford!

I remember well the journey south, spending my 21st birthday in the back of a 15 hundredweight wireless truck. Until October the regiment again occupied several localities in the Midlands along with the rest of the 18th division. Training as a division was intensified, especially with regard to improving the coordination between all the units in the division. It was now obvious to us that from now on things were going to be a bit more serious, the "Dad's Army time was now over". I remember on one occasion the artillery was tested at Larkhill on Salisbury plain, during which I remember vividly an incident involving our troop and a bevy of brass hats. The scene was a concrete bunker and the troop was engaging targets in the far distance with Captain Robinson and me directing fire. The usual method was employed of using one gun to latch on to the specific target, this proceeded quite well except when the first shell landed the captain turned to me and in a stage whisper enquired whether I had seen the shell burst. I certainly had but realising Robinson with his poor eyesight had not, I wrote down the necessary correction to line and range and surreptitiously passed it to him, thereupon with a loud and commanding voice he passed the necessary information down the phone. While this was going on the Army top brass were seated on their shooting sticks enjoying their sandwiches and their beverages from their hip flasks. Robinson duly made one or two more corrections (again I was helpful) and then feeling very sure of himself ordered a round of fire from the troop's four guns. We never really did see where three of the shells landed as one exploded about 4 yards in front of the bunker causing an extremely large amount of soil, stones and mud to come through the narrow windows of the bunker showering all and sundry; in fact the blast blew everyone onto the floor. As the dishevelled Army brass climbed to their feet the language was flowery and blasphemous but one chap, I think a major general, his face purple, picked up the phone and ordered the officer at the gun position to the phone. He, a Lieutenant, was demoted to second lieutenant and the sergeant on the offending gun was reduced to the rank of bombardier. I regret to say on looking around the bunker I had difficulty in concealing my laughter, but Robinson was a little more perturbed, after all, as a mere captain he could not appear to enjoy the situation.

Later on in the summer Helen, in one of her letters, told me that she was joining the women's auxiliary air force as at that time we were corresponding on a regular basis and before long she was ordered to report to the RAF training establishment at Bridgenorth. In the later period of her training we both managed to obtain passes and we met up for the day in Wolverhampton. It was great to see her and after a meal at the local branch of Toc H we went to the afternoon show at the Odeon cinema where we saw Cary Grant and Katharine Hepburn in a really marvellous comedy. It was a day we both never forgot, at the end of the day we went our separate ways with tears and I think that it was that day when we realised how much we meant to each other. The year went by and following the posting of a more senior Sergeant to the school of artillery I found myself promoted to the rank of Lance Sgt with the duty of controlling, from a survey point of view, the whole Unit, thus I parted from my association with dear captain Robinson, I did miss him! As part of my new duties I was required to ride a motorcycle and in due course I was handed a 500cc Norton motor cycle number 13 and told to get acquainted with it as soon as possible. This I did and became reasonably proficient despite biting the dust on a number of occasions; in fact the last spill occurred just before the machine was created for embarkation and as far as I know it was packed with several appendages flattened. I never saw it again; as things turned out probably some poor Oriental met his end riding it (especially if it had the number 13 still on it). Soon we were sent on embarkation leave which was as far as I can remember occurred in early September 1941. With a little bit of wrangling

I managed to obtain a travel warrant which allowed me to go from Stafford to London, then after three days, from London to Edinburgh and thence to Peebles, finally at the end of the leave back to Stafford. I had been able to arrange this itinerary as Helen had obtained leave to coincide with my going to Peebles in the latter half of my leave. I accordingly was able to say goodbye to my parents and have a wonderful time with Helen before a tearful parting. We at that time of course had no idea for certain as to where I was going and for how long I would be away although judging by the camouflage and equipment issued we were almost certain that we were bound for North Africa; how wrong would we be! The main thing that I did on that never to be forgotten leave was to propose to Helen though of course marriage would not be arranged until my return, which we both understood, avowing that we would be true to one another until that day came. The day before my leave ended we travelled into Edinburgh and at a small jewellers shop at the top of Leith Walk we purchased an engagement ring for the princely sum of nine pounds. Looking back to that incident which occurred over 70 years ago I recollect that I had great difficulty in raising the money and with embarrassment I prevailed upon Helen for a pound or two; luckily the jeweller also weighed in with the ring at sale price!

# Sailing to Hell

## 1941–1943

It was at the end of October 1941 that we embarked on the troop ship Orcades [about 23500 Gross Tonnage] belonging to the Orient steam navigation company and left for a destination unknown. I understood later that we became part of quite a large convoy and that our Division was spread over a number of ships. In view of the large number of troops and amount of equipment involved all the ships were capable of a speed round about 20 knots. I believe this was known as a fast convoy and as such should be capable of out running a U-boat. Therefore with convoys of this type, royal navy escorts were scaled down, at any rate on looking out to sea during daylight hours I saw only one or two destroyers. At that time of the year the Atlantic was pretty rough and at times the Orcades seemed to stand up on end causing most of the troops to spend their time violently sick, not many turning up at mealtimes. Luckily for me I must have inherited from my grandfather and uncle the ability of having a sturdy pair of sea legs, certainly my appetite didn't suffer. After the war it came to my knowledge that two months prior to our sailing, Winston Churchill and President Roosevelt had secretly met at Newfoundland and between them they had launched the Atlantic Charter. Following an attack by a U-boat on a United States destroyer in the following month it had been further agreed that United States Navy ships would be provided to carry British troops to the Middle East with an escort of U.S. warships . Apparently two Troopship Divisions comprising six transports sailed from American ports to rendezvous with our convoy at Halifax, Nova Scotia, on or about November 6, thus forming a group to be known secretly as "Convoy William Sail12X." Although war between Germany and the U.S.A. was not declared until the end of the year there is no doubt that in the minds of the top brass of Britain and America there was already an alliance between our two countries. Meanwhile our convoy was ploughing on but when we had more or less passed the halfway mark of the Atlantic crossing we were greatly surprised when a fairly large armada of warships took over from our puny escort of destroyers. More surprisingly was the appearance of a number of planes including Catalina flying boats and in the view of our distance from land the warships must have included an aircraft carrier. As the saying goes they were not ours but at least they were not firing at us, they must be American! Our passage across the north Atlantic had been pretty stormy and we were grateful when we finally steamed into Halifax.

After the blackout we had experienced in Britain for over two years I enjoyed standing on the deck in the evening looking at the strings of bright lights along the shore and at the main lights of the town. Such illumination, I thought to myself, might not be seen back home for some time to come, possibly not for many years. It was now November and at the end of the first week we were told that we were moving to a different ship and we were greatly surprised to find we were boarding a very large American liner. It turned out to be the Westpoint and we learned later that she was launched in 1939 as the cruise ship America but had been taken over by the US Navy in May

1941. Of course at that time we were all of the belief that we were being taken as reinforcements to the Middle East and with the Mediterranean being virtually closed we were in for a long voyage around the Cape of Good Hope. The Westpoint being about 40,000 tonnage accommodated pretty well a whole brigade. I can remember that we as an artillery group of 15 sergeants were in one large cabin fitted with steel bunks which was to be our home for almost three months. At the beginning of the second week in November the troop ships, with escorts, moved out from Halifax in the early hours of the morning; it was a great sight as the six transports surrounded by what appeared to be an aircraft carrier and about eight other warships made their way southwards with aircraft flying overhead. It would have been a brave U-boat commander to have approached that lot! Within an hour or two the convoy was more or less out of sight of land and what I remember most was the amount of air activity as planes patrolled ceaselessly over the convoy, with the escort of destroyers also speeding to and fro, you can't beat the Americans for putting up a show! And the Westpoint itself also was the subject of great interest to us and also the American crew who likewise were greatly interested in British soldiers whom probably they had never met before. To us their American accents all seemed the same but I think that the various regional accents of the British, for them proved very difficult – after all we were a mixture of Londoners, men from East Anglia and not to mention various Scots. Another source of amusement to us was the ships intercom system which in the main was meant for the crew but we found very enjoyable to listen to, with every announcement being preceded by "Now Hear This." After a few days we tended to chime in with "we are all ears."

A big point of interest was of course the food which was typical American prepared by American cooks and served up on trays with multiple compartments. A lot of it of course came out of tins but compared to British Army rations it took first prize; there was a lot of sweetcorn, chips and tinned fruit which we found enjoyable although the spiced pineapple had to be got used to. The amounts of food dished out were fairly large and we soon followed the American habit of only using a fork with which to eat, but of course there was always plenty of iced water and ice cream to hand. The convoy made its steady way down the East Coast of the United States and as we progressed the weather became more pleasant and although we did not know it at the time we were going to pass through the Caribbean and make our way to Trinidad.

I think the Americans were acutely aware of possible enemy submarine activity and blackout procedures were carried out at dusk and in the Caribbean area there was increased air activity. However at this time we in the British forces were very happy with our lot and took regular exercise to keep ourselves fit. In the evenings we played cards, lotto or even chess to keep ourselves occupied and on occasion had a singsong and of course in those days most people smoked and American cigarettes could readily be obtained. Eventually towards the end of November we anchored off the Port of Spain, Trinidad where I think we stayed for about two days, presumably to refuel and replenish stocks of food. Unfortunately shore leave was not allowed for anyone but it was quite pleasant to laze about in the sun. Now we knew precisely where we were and as we still believed we were going to North Africa it became obvious to us the direction our convoy would be going was towards the Cape of Good Hope before turning north towards the Persian gulf area. On leaving Trinidad we presumably followed the coast of South America but I cannot remember seeing anything but the open sea in all directions, however the weather was pleasant and for us despite drills and lectures it felt like a holiday. In my scrapbook which I compiled after the war I found I had kept a small certificate which had been printed on the Westpoint and which recorded the fact that on 23 November 1941 we had passed through the equator. It also stated that Davy Jones had come aboard on that day and that we had all been initiated by him into the Royal order of the Deep and had changed from landlubbers into Shell backs. As far as I can remember it was a great day, the war seemed far away and the evening ended with the usual singsong and drink, non-alcoholic of course.

By now we were crossing the South Atlantic and the boredom on the Westpoint was broken by arranging a boxing tournament between the British Army and the American crew, and although by now we all regarded ourselves as allies you would have thought that from the bouts that took place we were the deadliest of enemies. Every opponent was cheered to the hilt by his compatriots and every doubtful decision greeted with derision and of course a considerable number of side bets took place but I'm afraid I cannot remember what currency was used. I think the British overall won the contest, which to be fair they should have, as we outnumbered the Yanks considerably – although I distinctly remember my Battery Sgt Major, a big lad, being decisively beaten in the heavyweight class by a black American stoker who I can only describe as being enormous. At the end it was handshakes all round and all hostility put to bed! From the time when we crossed the equator (November 23, 1941) to when we docked in Cape

Town (December 9) the troops on board were not aware of any possible danger to the convoy and we were unaware of the attack by the Japanese on Pearl Harbour until we reached Cape Town. Since the war I have learned that the British government had prior knowledge of messages sent to U-boats as by that time they had broken the German codes. Accordingly they had the means to ensure that the convoy could be guided safely to its destination. In the few days before we reached Cape Town the weather got rougher and colder and I can only surmise that the convoy had gone quite a distance southwards and had approached the Port from the South. We were allowed ashore (probably 10th of December) for the day and it was great to enjoy the hospitality from the South African people. I myself managed to visit the office of the company I had worked for in Cheapside and they kindly sent a message back to their London office to be duly pass to my parents. After such a long time at sea we enjoyed walking around the town and seeing the thriving shops and brightly dressed people, after the darkened towns and rationing of Britain it seemed a different world. Unfortunately owing to mist we were not able to take the cable car up to the top of Table Mountain. It was during our short stay in Cape Town that it became apparent to most of us that the treatment of coloured people was not how it should have been; separate facilities were set aside for them which were in the main inferior. Mark you this had also been noticed by us on the American ships but maybe not quite to the same extent and personally I was very pleased that after the war this situation was righted even if it had taken far too long. Everyone of course, ourselves, the South African people, and I hope the Americans were happy that following Pearl Harbour we were all in the fight together, certainly on the Westpoint, the crew and ourselves seemed to have an increased sense of comradeship. About two days later after replenishment the Westpoint and others in the convoy left port for the next stage of our journey which we still mistakenly thought would be towards North Africa, how wrong would we be!

At this stage in the voyage we (at least the other ranks) were in the dark with regard to the progress of the Japanese Imperial Army, we did not know that the Japanese forces had penetrated a considerable way down the Malayan peninsula and there is no doubt that at that time, about one week of Japan entering the war, things were going very badly and consequently the government at home were in a quandary. I believe they were probably under pressure from the Australian government and Gen Percival, Commander of forces in Malaya, to send reinforcements and so reluctantly they had to change their plans regarding the use of the 18th Division. I think they still had hope that a fair part of the division could still be used in the Middle East and this possibly gave rise to the decision to send one brigade out of three direct to Singapore; the remainder being taken on to Bombay to await a further order. The convoy was accordingly split and I believe that escort duties were now principally in the hands of the British. It later transpired that the 53rd Brigade had been chosen to go direct whilst the 54th and ourselves the 55th in the Westpoint found ourselves on the way to Bombay. The next part of the journey took almost 2 weeks and as far as I can recall was fairly uneventful although we did notice that the number of escorts had decreased; however after docking in Bombay (now called Mumbai), we disembarked, I believe, in the early hours of the morning. We were allowed in the town for an hour or two and I know that apart from a little sightseeing I took the opportunity to send a cable from the main post office assuring folks back home that I was well and alive! Later that day we boarded a troop train which took us via Poona to Ahmadnagar about a hundred and fifty miles inland and it was at this point that we wondered whether we were going to spend a good part of the war in India, but again how wrong were we. At Ahmadnagar we found ourselves in a compact Army camp where we were well looked after and there is no doubt while we were there, for about three weeks, the government back home were uncertain as to whether or not we were to be pitched into the Malayan conflict. Finally we were moved back to Bombay, reboarded the Westpoint and proceeded at top speed to Singapore which we reached at the end of January. The dillydallying of the British government during our time in India prevented us from getting off Singapore Island and joining the 53rd Brigade on the Malayan peninsular. Possibly if this had been done at the outset the outcome of the conflict might have been different, but I doubt it. During this part of the voyage I remember that towards the end of it we passed through the Sunda Strait escorted by HMS Glasgow and although in the main the voyage was uneventful on one occasion HMS Glasgow opened fire on what they believed was a Japanese reconnaissance plane. History records that the withdrawal of the Commonwealth forces from the Malayan peninsula on to Singapore Island occurred on 30 January 1941 and as far as I can remember we (the 54th and 55th Brigades of the 18th division) had arrived in Singapore the day before. I suppose looking back on it now we had more or less entered a trap and that right from the start we were in a defensive situation and it was a case of hanging on as long as possible. After the war I think I read somewhere that even at the last minute Churchill had realised that committing the 18th division to the fray had been a mistake and that thought was given to diverting the remaining two brigades to Burma. However it is possible that again Australian opinion prevailed and as the ensuing battle for the Island proceeded the two brigades were never able to fight in the manner in which they had been trained and were condemned to 3 1/2 years of incarceration and suffering.

On landing we (the 55th Brigade) were transported up to the coastal sector on the North Eastern corner of the island facing out across the Johore Strait. The guns were dug in and command posts set up amongst the rubber tree plantations and I remember that almost immediately there was controversy as to whether we would be allowed to chop down rubber trees which were preventing a satisfactory field of fire. It's hard to believe that there could have been any argument of this nature at such a vital period of time but it would become clear after the war that a curious mentality did exist between the Army higher command and the civilian organisation prior to the Japanese invasion. I cannot remember much activity on our part from our initial position, while as I believe that there was little Japanese activity on the Johore shore in front of us, I would imagine at that time that most activity would be in and around the Causeway and Johore Bahru, an area being held by Indian and Australian troops who in the main were more experienced and better trained in battle. Whilst we were moving into our initial positions in the area of Seletar aerodrome, the transports which had brought us (including the Westpoint) had been loaded with refugees and evacuees to be transported safely to Ceylon calling in at Batavia in Java on the way to pick up even more refugees. Even after these ships had left, one or two ships still arrived bringing in the more traditional support troops including a detachment from the Northumberland Fusiliers, I believe about four days after we arrived. As you can imagine Singapore island was to a great extent overcrowded and with the bombing of the town and the dock area there was a great deal of congestion, also confusion coupled with a deal of panic. For us in the 118 Field Regiment life was comparatively peaceful, of course we could hear the bombing, see the smoke and hear the droning of the Japanese planes but there was hardly any activity at all in front of us, in fact the war seemed to be lacking a sense of urgency. As I stated before the 18th division was covering the coast of the island from the Causeway to Changi whilst the Australian troops covered from the Causeway around the West Coast to the small aerodrome at Tengah. The remainder of the island was covered to the south including the city limits of Singapore itself by Indian and Malayan troops including the Singapore volunteers. We also learned at this time that the last convoy which had arrived after us, round about 5 February, had been heavily bombed and the main ship the Empress of Asia had been sunk; this was a blow as a large quantity of Small Arms was lost. During this period (February 5th to February 9th) it would appear that nearly all artillery activity was on the west coast, therefore we with our 25 pounders of the 18th division were only firing sporadic shells over into Johore, not only was there a lack of targets but ammunition was limited. I believe that General Percival still considered that the main thrust from the enemy would come against the north coast area stretching from the Causeway eastwards. Increased shelling of the Australians positions on 8 February was followed by landings on the next day by Japanese forces in small boats against the

22nd Australian brigade who occupied the coast north of Tengah airfield. At about this time in the command post, I was engaged with others with the plotting of a possible barrage using most of the regimental guns aimed at the southern shore of the mainland opposite us, but for various reasons this was not proceeded with, probably one being due to the supply of ammunition and secondly precise identification of where the enemy actually were. This kept me busy and so when a communication came in from Royal Artillery headquarters in Singapore that the senior surveyor NCO should report to them immediately, I asked my commanding officer to send my deputy bombardier instead, great mistake! After the war I learned that the higher command had more or less decided Singapore was lost and had taken the opportunity to collect as many trained technicians as possible and put them aboard the last warship to leave for Columbo, Sri Lanka. In early 1946 I met one or two of the lads who had embarked on that last warship, now they were resplendent in their officers uniforms, didn't they do well! News as to what was happening on the west side of the island was kept from us (at least from the other ranks) so we were surprised when orders came to pull back into the northern suburbs of the town, where we established our command post in a spacious top-class bungalow. We had no idea at that time that things were going badly and that by 10 February the Japanese had reached the Bukit Timah village south of the Ford factory only five miles from the city centre. Apparently following fierce fighting, the Australians in the next two days pulled back to the city limits whilst on the south coast the Malay brigade had retreated even further back to Keppel harbour, we ourselves were still about five miles further north. As far as we were concerned by the 14th of February we as an artillery unit had not even seen a single Japanese and our activity consisted of sporadic firing in order to conserve the dwindling stocks of ammunition. We were not aware of the chaos that existed in Singapore itself, of the fires, bomb and shell damage, and not least the shortage of water. I believe on the 13th of February the last reservoir had come under the control of the Japanese.

In the evening of 15 February 1942 again to our surprise we were told that we had surrendered and that all steps should be taken immediately to render all equipment unusable; this we did to the best of our ability and we were lucky to find a well in one of the bungalow gardens into which we threw everything that would be of value to the enemy. Later that evening and early the following morning most of us spent our time scrounging as we were apprehensive as to what the future would hold for us and exactly where our next meal would come from. The surrounding bungalows were searched and a quantity of tinned food was found and stowed away in our Army packs; following which we shaved and waited for the next move of the Japanese. I think it was about midday when they appeared and for the first time since 1939 when I walked into the offices of the Mitsui Company in the city of London I again was face-to-face with a Japanese person. I think we were surprised at their appearance which to us seemed scruffy and not in any sense military in that except for old-fashioned looking rifles they did not have a great deal of equipment. This left us with a feeling and question as to how we could have surrendered to such an opponent and I think that this was reflected later on in our attitude to the top brass in our Army. The Japanese force which came into our lines acted in a reasonable manner, their officers were more neatly uniformed, complete with sword, and had complete control over their men so that apart from them giving orders to our own officers, we were not harassed in anyway. The next day we were marched from our position (South East of the Mac Ritchie reservoir) to the main Singapore to Changi road in the North Chinatown area, where we lined up on the roadside along with thousands more prisoners of war. This afforded Gen Yamashita and his entourage the opportunity to drive in state, passed lines of the defeated enemy to satisfy his sense of importance and of course for the benefit of the cameras. Following which we turned to the North East guarded by lines of Japanese soldiers and armoured vehicles and marched towards Changi about five miles away. The first two or three miles of the road were lined by Chinese and Malaysian onlookers waving obvious standard issue paper Japanese flags, whilst in the main part the Chinese looked distinctly glum, the Malays tended to jeer, these jeers were replied to by we the British gunners, with the customary two digit salute, after all we were a regiment from south-east London and cockneys from that part don't take things lying down. In due course we reached the Changi barracks area feeling very weary and were allocated accommodation following which the area was barbed wired and the majority of the Japanese guards disappeared. I think that it was at this point the British officers decided that it was necessary to regain control of their troops and they made it quite clear that from that time on discipline had to be re-established. I personally had no quarrel with this decision, but later on I would wish that their concern for troops under their control would have been more to the fore when we were involved in the building of the Siam – Burma railway, when in an incident, I came to realise that any concern for other ranks in their regiment was definitely lacking.

It took a little time before things at Changi got organised, for a while fresh water was rationed (the reservoirs on the island had been damaged by bombing) and the feeding of the prisoners and the supply of food had to be established. When supplies of food eventually turned up it consisted in the main of rice and some vegetables, not exactly grub which would satisfy our palates and we in our unit were grateful that in the few hours before the surrender we had taken the opportunity to find some tins of fish and meat etc which we now had with us. Although through the summer we were left to our own devices the Japanese from time to time called for various work parties and I remember that on one occasion a group of us were taken back to the outskirts of the town and were employed in the breaking up of civilian cars that had been left behind by their owners who had been evacuated. A Japanese NCO on discovering I could drive, put me in an armoured car which had no turret, and I was instructed to drive it at the rows of cars at full speed thus breaking them up very quickly into more manageable bits; I found this great fun! Of course the more useful parts of engines etc had been previously removed and as I was in this work party for some time I was eventually moved into a large hut where under the supervision of a nice Japanese man (about the only one) I worked on sorting out car components into size and make and stacking them in order on the shelves (a promotion?). The Jap and I got on quite well, of course he had no English and I had no Japanese but sign language worked very well and I gathered that he came from Tokyo and worked before the war as a porter in the fish market, but then on reflection I may have been mistaken! A

Chinese individual who also worked in the store, I think was not very happy at being left out of the picture and on occasion took the opportunity to make it known to my Japanese friend that he considered my work to be unsatisfactory. I'm glad to say he was rewarded by a heavy blow to his head; I don't think the Japanese are altogether too fond of the Chinese! Before I returned to the confines of Changi I remember another incident which occurred in the car industry which concerned a number of us driving about a dozen serviceable cars down to the docks for shipment. In order to save petrol they were lined up behind each other joined by short ropes with the first car acting as a tower, the other 11 only being steered. Off we went and things went well until about a mile from the docks, going downhill, an Indian policeman spotted a Japanese officer coming out of a side road in a military car. Immediately he stepped into the road about 9 feet from the towing car which pulled up about 6 inches from his chest with a scream of brakes, but unfortunately the 11 cars behind had no chance and like railway trucks they bashed into each other with a glorious tinkle of glass and battered metal. We all considered this keystone cops episode extremely funny and laughed like hell but we were soon brought to earth when the Japanese officer ordered us to kneel at the side of the road in a line and put our heads on the kerb. Our worries increased when he unsheathed his sword but apart from waving it about and shouting at us we were subsequently allowed to get to our feet and resume our journey but I'm pleased to say that the member of the Indian National Army received an extremely hard clout from the officer. This work party concerning vehicles did not last very long for me and it was the only one I went on during the remainder of the year although many other work parties did go into Singapore to work in the dock area. There was one extraordinary activity which did occur early in our captivity when a cricket match was arranged with the Australians who, in normal circumstances were in a different area from ourselves. The guards by this time were mainly from the Indian National Army so permission must have been granted for this game to go on and in due course it was billed as a test match for the Ashes. I was roped in to make up the England side and it cheered us up enormously when with the aid of one of the Edrich family from Norfolk and two Lancashire League players we beat the Aussies, who had on their side Ben Barnett a Test wicket-keeper batsman. As far as I can remember it was played on a matting wicket, with a shortage of top class equipment, but victory was sweet and was achieved without yours truly having to bat. By this time most of our regiment were billeted inside Singapore Gaol and along with other units we were crammed into the cells and the communal rooms. Four gunners and myself occupied one cell which was about 8' x 6' in size with a stone sleeping slab in the centre, and being the NCO I took this and the four lads settled in around it. Toilet and water facilities did not exist and with the gates and doors being always open these facilities were outside the Gaol, as were a number of huts made of wood and thatched with palm leaves which were also used for accommodation and for medical purposes. At this time in the summer of 1942 work parties for our own benefit were organised in the camp, one of them being the collection of wood for cooking and another, cultivation of certain areas within the camp to provide some sort of vegetable to be used to make the rice more palatable. Rations at this time were getting distinctly poorer and every effort had to be made to make life more tolerable. I myself worked in the gardens for some time as the principal NCO under a young Indian Army lieutenant named Scott Russell and I believe we were reasonably successful in producing a quantity of green crops (mainly green and red amaranth) in the poor soil. As these gardens were at a distance from the camp we had with us a guard who supervised the distribution of the garden implements which were kept under lock and key at the garden, presumably to prevent them being used as some sort of weapon. It was my job to check them in and check them out and there was hell to pay if numbers did not tally; if this should happen as it did on a number of occasions a few guards would arrive and distributed a number of beatings. After all these years I still have a list in an old notebook of the implements (in number over 250) for which I was responsible and when I say there were about 26 varieties ranging from 29 chungkols (heavy) down to one cross cut saw you can imagine that at times I was not a happy lad. Thinking back to that time I seem to remember that one of our lads, when the Japanese guard was not looking, did some sketching. At the time I felt that he was not pulling his weight but since he had the approval of Scott Russell I thought no more about it and after the war I came to the conclusion it was Ronald Searle.

However we did find a little relaxation on one or two evenings when we had a few card games together for an hour or two. My particular friends on these occasions were Stan Evans and Ernie Kirtley and if I remember correctly we were joined by a Nigel Carruthers (who had been in the Singapore volunteers) to make up the foursome, the game of course being bridge. At that time I was also great friends with Norman Deroza and Laurie Van der Stratten both also having been in the Singapore volunteers. Nigel was a great friend and when he learned that I was engaged to a Scots girl from Peebles he told me that his family had an estate at Lockerbie, and should I be looking for a job after the war, he gave me a letter addressed to his brother, who would give me as much help as possible. As things turned out later I did not need to use the letter and some years after the war I read in a newspaper that the family mansion at Lockerbie had been given to the Royal engineers for practice purposes. Nigel, before the fall of Singapore, I believe was connected with the Ford factory in Malaya and it was with regret that I lost touch with him following our movement to Thailand to work on the infamous railway. However recently in this computer age I was able to ascertain that after a spell staying on in Singapore he returned to Lockerbie and eventually died in 1984, he was without doubt a great gentleman. As time passed by we were all getting much thinner on our daily meagre rations of rice and vegetable stew and diseases such as ulcers and beriberi became more frequent and in addition at the end of summer there occurred what was known to us as the Selarang incident. A prominent Japanese general decided that all POWs would sign a declaration in which they would promise that in no circumstance would they try to escape. Our own officers quoting the Geneva Convention turned the Japanese order down flat and this action was followed by all prisoners of war being shepherded to the Selarang barrack area where we were to remain without food and sanitary facilities until we did sign. The area was quite small and with just under 20,000 troops one could say it was pretty crowded and after two or three days we were all in poor condition and the smell also left a great deal to be desired! Things got so bad that our officers finally agreed that we could sign under duress although I personally could not see what the argument was all about since everyone knew that anyone who escaped and was caught was executed contrary to the Geneva Convention, which the Japanese did not recognise; any piece of paper they might later produce to justify their actions would be unlikely in turn not to be recognised. However unbeknown to us at that time it would appear that following the defeat of the Japanese Navy at the Battle of Midway and the probable inability of the their Navy to guarantee the safety of Japanese merchant ships operating in the seas around Rangoon a decision had been taken to build the Thai-Burma rail link. It may well be that if thousands of POWs were moved into Thailand the Japanese might have worried about a large number of escapes taking place and that the signing of the forms would give them the excuse to carry out executions.

The planning of the Thai-Burma railway, according to information after the war, had been initiated by Japanese engineers in March 1942 and in the late summer of that year the majority of us were not aware that an initial force of Australians had been moved to southern Burma to commence work on the railway from the Burmese end. It also transpired that thousands of Asian labourers had also been transported to Thailand and had commenced working on the railway sometime before the movement of prisoners from Singapore. By October 1942 probably 20,000 British POWs had been moved to Thailand and later on when the railway became a matter of urgency for the Japanese the workforce was reinforced by thousands more by Dutch P.O.Ws from Java and by scraping more prisoners from Singapore. If we now thought that the situation in Changi with regard to food and medical facilities had been getting worse, little did we know what suffering there was now before us. In the best part of a year we all suffered from malnutrition and there had been many deaths. The Red Cross not having been recognised meant that we had received no comforts whatsoever and to date not a postcard or letter had arrived from home. We that were still alive, wondered if folks at home knew whether we were alive, although after several months we had been allowed to send one printed postcard, no cards had been received by us, thus raising doubts as to what had happened with the cards we had sent. I personally had made an allowance from my pay to my mother which had only been paid by the British paymaster for a number of months in the hope that I was still alive. Presumably if he had received news to the contrary then repayment would have been demanded! Thus we were approaching a time in our imprisonment that would test our resolve and desire to the utmost, survive many of us would not make it, either through despair or simple bad luck. My turn would come to suffer and endure hardship and there would be times during the building of the railway and even later, when like everyone else it would seem there was no hope of release and getting home. Even if the fortunes of war had turned in favour of the Allies the final struggle we felt would end in our execution. These thoughts I know caused many a comrade to simply lie down and give up the fight. To get through you simply had to have the will to live and hope that sometime in the future a light at the end of the tunnel would appear.

# THE RAILWAY OF DEATH

## 1943–1944

The large batch of prisoners that had been moved up to Thailand in October and November 1942 were preceded by a smaller batch of Australians who had left Singapore in May 1942 destined for the Burma end of the railway. Another small batch of prisoners had also left towards the end of June 1942 and they were destined to set up the workshops and base at the Thailand end at a place called Nong Pladuk. I myself was not detailed for the force that had left Singapore at the end of 1942, so in a way that was a piece of luck, in that I continued working in the Changi area along with the remainder of the troops still left there, and at that time we saw very little of the Japanese guards. We had no knowledge of what was happening to those who had started work on the railway and mistakenly thought at the time that they were having a better time than we were, that was a long way from the truth! Christmas came and went (as far as the Japanese were concerned the only holiday they recognised was the Emperor's birthday). I can't remember that it was anything special except possibly the cooks endeavoured to make the rice more palatable and it was a time that made us think of friends and family. The number of comrades who were getting sick was on the increase and consequently the number of deaths rose, even those of us who were still reasonably fit were losing weight. By this time we still had not received letters or postcards from home and to our knowledge the one or two printed cards we had been allowed to fill in may still be languishing in Singapore. The first few months of 1943 went by and in March we learned that we were also going to Thailand and of course according to the Japanese it was going to be a holiday, with the food being a lot better, providing we did a lot of work for our lord and master! Accordingly with whatever kit we had (most of us just had what we stood up in) we were paraded and marched to Singapore station for the rail journey to Thailand. If we expected a train with carriages we were a little disappointed, a line of steel wagons awaited us, metal doors pulled back and in we got 30–35 to the truck.

Almost 67 years later I would be able to extinguish the disappointment and foreboding of that day by getting aboard the Eastern and Oriental express and making the same journey in luxury. At this time we had no idea as to the fate of the parties that had left Singapore before our particular group. Apparently just before we left Singapore a party called D force had left to work on the part of the railway which was situated roughly in the centre of the Thailand section and our party labelled F force was destined for the following section up to the Burma border. The movement of these two forces had resulted in the number of POWs left in Changi down to a matter of hundreds – in fact some of the men on F force were already in a very unfit state of health. My knowledge of the layout of the railway then was very sketchy but after the war I learned that it ran from Ban Pong (the junction of the existing railway to Bangkok) through virgin jungle up to the border with Burma and then on to Thanbyuzayat (the junction of the existing railway to Moulmein). It would seem that the first 50 km from the depot at Ban Pong to Kanchanaburi had been constructed by Thai labourers and that the first batch of POWs who left Singapore at the end of 1942 had been put to work on the following section up to Wang Pho, a total distance of 114 kilometres. In March 1943 (at this time the Allied naval forces were fighting back) the Japanese considered that the railway had become even more important, and therefore the D Force sent at that time would work on the section from Wang Pho up to Kinsaiyok, now making a total distance so far of approximately 172 km.

We now come to the force of which I had become a member, a force known by the letter F, in more ways than one, very appropriate. Our work would take us on to the final part of the Thai section as far as the Burma border at The Three Pagodas, making a total distance to that point about 305 km, so that, including the Burma section being built the total railway, was in the region of 415 km long. However this was all in front of us as we climbed into the wagons at Singapore station helped along by shouts and by jabs from rifle butts and duly squatted on the metal floors. In due course metal doors clanged shut and it was an hour or two before the train moved off, and by that time the sweat was pouring off us, the only air coming into the wagon was through a small gap between the two doors. We made ourselves as comfortable as possible but with about 36 men in the confined space this required fitting bodies like pieces of a jigsaw puzzle and when aching muscles and limbs became unbearable, movement was extremely difficult. However we took it in turns to stand by the gap in the doors to get a breath of fresh air and to get a view of what was happening outside. Of course toilet facilities did not exist, we simply had to wait for the train to stop when we were allowed off the train for a meal of rice and thin stew which occurred twice a day; as you may surmise this did not always meet our needs and the atmosphere in the truck after time got rather unpleasant. As far as I can remember this hell of a journey took the best part of five days until we arrived at the appropriately named Ban Pong, where we left one pong or smell for another. Urged on by the Japanese and Korean guards with a great deal of shouting and waving of rifles we disembarked from the railway wagons, were marched to a large warehouse for a day's rest and a meal of soggy rice and stew.

During this time a search was made of our belongings and we were subject to a cursory medical inspection in which the main test was the taking of our temperatures by inserting a thermometer into our back passage. We were not furnished by any result or reading so presumably we were A1! In the weeks to come our knowledge of what was happening on the railway gradually grew through contact with prisoners who had gone before us, although contact and conversation between different groups of POWs was forbidden, and anyone caught was severely beaten. It became apparent to us that diseases of various kinds had affected working parties very badly, including Asian labourers and that our party were in a way replacements for casualties. We learned later that the main cause of POW deaths was dysentery caused by food and water being contaminated by infections carried in most cases by flies. Deaths were also caused by cholera, to a lesser extent by beriberi, malaria, diarrhoea and tropical ulcers and of course, malnutrition which did not help at all. It became very obvious to me in the months that followed that hygiene played a large part in keeping one alive, there was no doubt that lack of proper sanitary arrangements was responsible for the greater number of deaths suffered by the Asian labourers. British and Australian POWs were very conscious that all water required to be boiled and latrines should be dug and used away and below sleeping and cooking areas. This unfortunately was not carried out by other nationalities. After the brief stop in Ban Pong we started on foot towards our camp on the railway, little did I know it would involve a march of about 300 km, at the end of which the work I had to do made me extremely thankful that I had a pair of strong legs, developed in my late teens by my athletic training. When we set off, the road was reasonably dry and we made quite good progress; we also carried the kit that we had brought from Singapore but later on as some POWs got weaker, a lot of articles were dumped by the wayside.

During our march we passed camps that were already established but we were not allowed to go into them, presumably the Japanese did not want any contact by us with workers already on the railway, it would have brought to light the appalling conditions which existed in these established camps. However we did get our two meals of rice each day so no doubt these were brought out from such camps. The monsoon had not yet broken and the weather was dry and very hot so the guards who were also feeling the heat tended to call a halt in the middle part of the day and extend the marching into the evening. I would estimate that initially we may have covered possibly 16 km per 24-hours but of course as many POWs got weaker this rate of progress deteriorated despite being urged on by blows and shouts. Later on when the road became nothing more than a dirt track and we got the odd downpour of rain things became even more difficult and to make things easier many prisoners dumped even the last articles of their belongings and simply crawled on in what they stood up in. Eventually in the final stages of the march many of the prisoners lagged behind and despite goading by the guards they simply did not have the strength to go any further. My only hope was that they were taken into the nearest camp but I have doubts on that score. At night we slept on the ground, those of us that still had a ground sheet were lucky, otherwise you took your chance with the things that were crawling on the ground, but we were too tired to worry about scorpions, snakes or anything else that moved.

We had no knowledge of what was happening in the camps we passed by; we were not aware that prisoners were dying in them from numerous diseases and of course cholera was rife. I think that we must have been on the march for more than two weeks when we finally marched into the camp which was to be our home for the next six months, its name I eventually learned was Kami Songkurai. The camp was already occupied by Australian prisoners of war and at that time I think it was known to them as number three camp as some of their comrades were already working at the main Songkurai (No 2) and Shimo Songkurai (No 1) camps. Our camp as far as one could see lay in a fairly flat valley which was covered with high dense bamboo and apparently was smaller in size than the other two camps at Songkurai. It was also situated 5 km below the Burma border at Three Pagodas Pass, thus we were pretty well the furthest from both ends of the railway. Our main job turned out to be building up an embankment to carry the railroad when it arrived and later on to provide the ballast for a distance of about 5 km in each direction. In addition there were small streams to be bridged and the cutting of timber and bamboo. These tasks in normal circumstances would have been arduous but we had left Singapore in a poor state physically and we were further exhausted by the long march we had just made. To make matters worse the situation of our camp meant that food supplies being sent to us I believe, were pilfered as they made their way up to us past the camps lower down, the Japanese guards being the main culprits.

The accommodation in the camp consisted of long bamboo huts roofed with atap (Palm Leaf), with bamboo platforms on either side and normally we had a small fire going on the floor in the middle. This was necessary as at night it became bitterly cold despite the overwhelming heat during the day. Kitchens for the cooking of rice were in separate huts and of course there was a hospital hut for the ill and those, who frankly were dying. The hospital was simply another hut with platforms, no equipment and no medicines, with the food ration for its inmates reduced in quantity by the Japanese, coupled with the exhortation "no work, no food". Work on the embankment was carried out from dawn to dusk and we were normally split into small gangs of six working in three pairs; two pairs worked filling sacking stretched between bamboo poles with earth, which they then carried to the top of the embankment for the third pair to spread and tread down. This task became harder as the embankment was built up, especially when it rained. I personally was thankful again for my strong legs, as many of my comrades the task became almost impossible in the wet mud, the amount of physical effort needed to lift the wet earth to a height of about 3m time after time the whole day was soul destroying. The building of the embankment was the initial priority and at that time in May 1943 the Japanese were not satisfied with the rate of progress being made. Bearing in mind that the completion of the railway was essential for the supply of materials to their troops in

Burma, the long journey by sea being taken at that time was threatened by Allied submarines. Accordingly extra labour forces were brought in as late as June in order to try and get the railway in operation by the end of the year; of course extra labourers were required to replace men dying in considerable numbers at most of the camps.

One of the worst camps for casualties was No 2 at Songkurai just 6 km below our camp where I found out later that more than a third of the POWs had died earlier in the year, mainly from cholera. On one occasion a party of us was detailed under guard to go to No 2 camp to bring back about half a dozen sacks of rice which were badly needed. The journey was made on foot and carrying the rice on our backs was very hard work but what I saw at that camp made me thankful that on our march to our own camp we had passed it by. We were given a little time to rest before making the return journey and I took the opportunity to surreptitiously call on three or four British officers comfortably established in a tent. One of the officers was from my own regiment and I thought they would all be interested in the up-to-date news of the other ranks from our camp. I was mistaken, they were not, they made it plain that I was interrupting their game of cards so I sadly left. Apparently the Japanese, in this camp, were not forcing officers to work but I felt that at least these officers should have been standing by their men and looking after them during working hours. At this camp there was a fairly large tributary running down into the main river, this required the building in wood of a trestle bridge. This bridge unlike the one at Kanchanaburi would be more like the one in the film "Bridge on the River Kwai" but of course this was not built with the help of a mad Colonel! The bridge at Kanchanaburi was promoted as the bridge in the film by the Thai tourism authorities as of course it is more accessible and is adjacent to the war cemetery and the recently established museum. Thus a complete tourist package was made available since in any case most of the railway has long disappeared, the jungle growing back and any bridges rotting away.

The Australians in our camp had their own huts and formed their own parties for work but of course many times we were working on adjacent parts of the railway. We were all underfed and not very happy with life but that did not stop us from indulging in the usual banter with them and in a way this made life more bearable and enabled us to let off steam, but believe me the language at times could be very ripe, if there had been any spare energy there would have been a fight or two! As the weeks went by it was obvious that the Japanese engineers were being more and more pressurised to complete the railway before the end of the year and accordingly, we the POWs, were driven even harder at work with threats and of course beatings. The hospital hut was raided by the Japanese engineers with patients who could walk being driven out to work. Each day brought a number of deaths in the camp mainly now from dysentery, malaria and beri-beri and of course the bodies had to be disposed of. This unfortunately, on occasion, meant an additional task on our return from the day's work. When my turn came round for doing this job I could hardly stomach the evening rice ration. We had to place the naked bodies on bamboo stretchers, having retained any scraps of clothing for future use, then make our way to a small clearing away from the camp. At the clearing there was a supply of bamboo together with dry kindling, the dog tags were removed and the bodies burnt, I cannot remember whether the ashes were interred and the spot marked, all I know is that years later that task never leaves my memory. Apart from the embankment several small streams had to be bridged in our area and this was done by cutting hardwood from the nearby jungle and using stone culverts to allow water to pass under the bridges. As far as I can remember we more or less had the embankment and the small bridges completed by September and about that time we were occasionally sent into the jungle to cut bamboo. This was not a very easy task as the parangs (similar to machetes) we used were not very sharp and the bamboo was very tall and held together at the top by vines. However this was a welcome break from constructing the railway and it was an opportunity to get a little friendly with the guards.

The Japanese soldier tends to be a bit boastful and although language was difficult we did on occasions have a laugh (between the occasional beating!). The opening gambit by the guard was normally uttered through his row of gold teeth as follows, "Tojo number one, Churchill number 99" (higher the number signified less status) a statement in view of the circumstances we chose not to disagree with. However knowing the Japanese respect for virility we would point to one of our lads and make it clear that he was the father of 12 children and if the guard was convinced then we would add with a laugh "England number one, Nippon number 99" which caused even the little bugger to laugh. On one other occasion on one of our rare breaks in some way the topic got round to athletics and the guard uttered the word "Olympic" following which we pointed to a rather short member of our gang and indicated that he was No 1 at high jump. The guard was not having this and erected a thin piece of bamboo at about a height of just over 1 metre and proceeded to run at it at the rate of an express train. Needless to say he cleared it with ease and then made it clear that our unfortunate comrade was to do the same. At first we tried to persuade the guard that we were happy with his performance and it was time to get back to work, but he was not having it and demanded our man earned the title of Number 1. I shall never forget the look on the guard's face when our man made his attempt and only rose about 1 foot off the ground and knocked the bar down with his shins, which in our opinion was a bloody good attempt bearing in mind his physical condition. I am pleased to say that we all reacted with laughter and calls of "number 99", in which the guard joined in (we were very happy to observe that he was not aware he had been made to look a fool). On the general subject of Japanese and Korean guards and their attitude to us I always found that if you could get only one or at the most two away from the main body of guards and their NCOs a sense of humour could be found, even if with difficulty.

Physical violence existed in the Japanese army and it seemed that every soldier had the right to beat the living daylights out of any comrade of inferior rank and when such incidents occurred they were normally done when other soldiers were present and that punishment had to be seen to be done. The work of building up the railway embankment continued up to about September 1943 and during the following month work parties were engaged in breaking up stone for ballast, it being anticipated that the track laying gang moving south from Burma would soon be with us. The provision of ballast came from a small shallow quarry not far from the camp and was extracted by means of hammers and chisels with the occasional use of explosives. The Australians and British were made up into gangs of 15-20 POWs and it was our job each day for each gang to make a pile of ballast, each heap to measure 5 m x 3 m and had to meet the approval of the Japanese engineer. It was hard work with sore hands and backs and if stone chips from the hammering pierced the skin there was a possibility of ulcers developing. No gang was allowed back to camp until the required heap had been made and initially all gangs were still working at dusk. If the Japanese engineers were not satisfied the usual beatings duly followed. However, after a time the floor of the quarry was quite full of the heaps of ballast and it became apparent to the British POWs that the Australian gangs were beginning to meet the targets quite some time before dusk. We smelled a rat and on observation it became obvious that they were dispensing with the breaking up of stone and moving ballast off existing piles. On the premise that what is good for the goose is also good for the gander everyone joined in on the ploy and the ballast piles simply moved around the quarry. However all good things come to an end and when the Japanese realised what was happening there was hell to pay, with whackings galore! Within a few weeks the track gang from Burma went past us and we were employed on ramming in the ballast between the sleepers. I learned later that at about the beginning of November the track laying gang from Burma had met the gang moving up from Thailand at a place called Konkoita, and that the incident had been celebrated with the knocking in of a gold spike.

By now the heavy rains were tapering off and we were only subject to the occasional heavy shower and our work more or less consisted of bamboo cutting and ballast laying and it was about this time that I suffered from a bout of dysentery. In no way would I report sick as from what I had observed, if you went into the medical hut the chances were that you never came out. On one occasion back in Singapore I had been told that a possible cure was eating charcoal and this I did by picking up pieces out of the fire in the hut, of course it was not very pleasant but after a week it did the job. A particular friend of mine Sgt Ron Breacher had gone into the hospital about a month ago and was now in a very poor state and I always remember a visit to see him. I did my best to cheer him up and as we were about to go back down the line, I assured him that I would pay him another visit before I left. This I did but he was in a very sorry state, very emaciated, suffering from dysentery and I felt the outlook was bleak; it was unlikely I would see him again. Exactly 66 years later when visiting the POW Museum at Kanchanaburi I found out for certain that he had died. On examining a burial list of all my comrades in the 118th Field Regiment Royal Artillery who had died on the railway, I discovered that whereas most of them were buried in the cemetery near the museum, those who had died at our camp had been taken over the border and buried in Burma. At the time of my visit to Thailand in 2009 it was difficult to get into Burma and therefore it was with regret that I was unable to pay due respects to his grave. It was late November when we were put on a train with flat-top wagons to travel down the track to the base camp/hospital at Kanchanaburi. The journey from our camp back to the base camp, a distance of about a 250 km, proved to be a hair raising experience owing to trucks coming off the rails, and of course it was our manual labour that put them back on again. We were lucky that on every occasion this happened we were on a level piece of the railway and not when we were going over a trestle bridge.

The large camp at Kanchanaburi was being used by the Japanese to sort out their POW labour force but one thing occurred which raised my spirits. I received my first mail from home since the short time we were in India, almost 2 years ago, and it consisted of two printed postcards both from my dearest Helen. Hardly any news but they expressed love and were from home, that's all I needed. At Kanchanaburi food and medical facilities were better, they could hardly be worse, and in view of the condition of the POWs from the work camps, the number of deaths still continued to mount, accordingly a month or two passed by before the Japanese considered splitting up and moving the workforce. This they did by retaining a considerable number to service the railway, many were sent back up the line for this work. Of the remainder whom they considered (in their eyes) reasonably fit at the time, half were sent back by rail to Singapore, and half over a short period of time were sent by sea to Japan. In retrospect I think I was lucky in being sent back to Changi in Singapore as at the end of the war I discovered that thousands of those destined for Japan had been drowned owing to the activity of Allied submarines. Books have been written telling of the sufferings of POWs who were unlucky enough to be shipped to Japan, many were to end their lives in shark infested seas, and even when they got to Japan hazardous mining work was their lot with only basic food. Again the policy of the Japanese to ignore the Geneva Convention by not marking the ships with the Red Cross symbols added to the POW death total. And so at the turn of the year we again climbed into the steel wagons in our groups of about 36 and made the tiring journey over five or six days back to Singapore. The journey was just as soul destroying as before, unhygienic, wearying, with lack of water and food and there was a sense of relief when we finally got back. It seemed to us when making the journey by road from Singapore station to Changi that there was a different atmosphere in the people we passed on the way; it was evident that they knew matters were not going so well with Japan and its allies in the outside world. At Changi this time we were put into huts outside the Gaol and after a brief interlude work parties were made up each day to carry out tasks the Japanese considered essential. Again food seemed to be in short supply; there were the usual two small meals a day of rice but little else, perhaps now and then a little watery stew. Before long all of us had lost more weight, which emphasised the skeleton look. From now on it seemed that we would be worked until we dropped, the chief enemy apart from the Japanese, would be malnutrition. The remainder of 1944 definitely would be hard going and the will to live would become essential. As far as Jack Ransom was concerned the part of his life involved with the Thai – Burma railway was now at an end, thank God and never to be forgotten. How could it be? There had been suffering, cruelty, at times starvation and finally the deaths. I survived but still there was a long way to go, maybe the worst might be over but as it later transpired a number of those who got back to Singapore still died before the end of the war. 1943 was now at an end, 1944 and onwards would see the war turning against Japan and I think they realised it. In the future we would be allowed to send one or two postcards back home which on receipt created a feeling of all is well, but the happiness of lots of families would disappear when in fact many POWs who were alive in 1944 did not survive to the end.

Asian labourers at work (these were employed initially but high mortality rate led to their withdrawal).

Trestle Bridge (these were constructing from teak hauled from the jungle by elephants).

Railway cutting (these were dug manually by pick and shovel, any rock was blasted away)

Three tier bridge (if you were working on this you did not drop your hammer!)

Completed railway (completed at the end of 1943 – limited use
owing to subsequent bombing)

Derailment: on my return from the Three Pagodas Pass back to base this was a great worry!

1941 – Helen and Jack

1950 – "Peebles" – Helen and Jack

1990 – Weston-super-Mare – Joyce and Jack

2009: Kranji Memorial, Singapore

2009: Kranji War Cemetary

I visit Ruffles Hotel, Singapore

On the Eastern Oriental Express

Taking it easy in the train bar

Up for a dance!

Graham and I enjoying Bangkok

The massage parlour girls, Bangkok

The Americans and Jack in the Bamboo Bar

Maddie and I on the Big Day, 2010

1920 – Peckham, London – baby Jack

2013 – Largs, Scotland – Maddie and Jack
93 years and still going strong!

# THE END GAME

## 1944–1945

After a few months there was greater activity on the part of the Japanese in that any civilians who had been in Changi Gaol were moved out and all POWs were moved inside the prison wall. Presumably this was done for greater security and was probably linked, although we did not know it at the time, to the fact that the Japanese forces had got bogged down in Burma, with the British forces on the point of fighting back. What was also apparent at the time was the continuing success of the Americans in the Pacific Islands. So once again I was back in a cell with another four comrades. I reckon in all, there must have been about 10,000 POWs within the confines of the outer wall of the gaol, and bearing in mind that it had been constructed originally to accommodate about 600 criminals, you can imagine that getting us in proved a very tight fit. I suppose in a way we were happier (if that term could be used) being back at Changi where we were away and out of sight of the Japanese guards (except when we were sent on working parties). But now malnutrition continued and many were increasingly suffering from diarrhoea, eye trouble and muscular deterioration. What troubled most POWs was that they could not see any light at the end of the tunnel, how would it end? Would the war last for years as the guards would predict from time to time? Or would there be at some time in the future hand-to-hand fighting in Singapore, in which case our execution would precede it. These thoughts of desperation coupled with illness caused many to simply lay down and die but I'm glad to say that most of us had no thought of giving up hope. It was just before the middle of 1944 that those of us who had some vestige of energy left were organised into work gangs for the specific construction of a military airbase in the Changi area. This again was a dawn to dusk job and once again it was labour with primitive tools, there were no modern lorries or bulldozers available and when we arrived back at the end of the day all we could do would be to consume our rice ration and fall asleep on the floor of our cell. The job of changing a large area of Changi into an airbase would have been an enormous task for a modern construction company with modern machinery so it appeared to us that the Japanese using POWs with only hand tools, shall we say, "were up against it". Every reasonable fit POW from time to time was engaged in this work as I believe that the Japanese demanded a workforce every day of about 1000 men. Another main workforce demanded by the Japanese was one (about half the size of the one on the airbase) to be transported down to the docks and railway station to move military stores of all types. This second work party was deemed by most of us to be the more desirable of the two but unluckily yours truly never managed to get on it, so my days in 1944 and into 1945 were spent in the heat and dust of the sandy waste of the airport. The work was backbreaking, digging, levelling, moving earth to fill up depressions and all done with spades and wheelbarrows in the glaring sun and heat of the day, plus of course the usual exhortations to work harder with the follow up of beatings. We had one meal of rice which we had taken out with us and of course we needed water all the time which had to be boiled in old 4 gallon petrol tins before use. Small areas of the airfield which were completed first were used almost immediately by the Japanese. I remember that down one particular parameter of the field there was a line of Zero fighters already parked, and doubtless when the airfield was completed it would hold several squadrons of fighter planes for the defence of Singapore. Apart from these two main work parties men were also required for duties necessary to keep the cook houses producing the meals, such as they were, for all the POWs. Fires had to be kept going under the large iron vessels used for cooking the rice, and thus work parties were sent out to cut timber (mainly rubber trees) and to haul it back to camp on trailers towed by the POWs themselves. As each month passed by it seemed that the allowance of rice was getting even smaller and I remember that on one occasion the rice supplied by the Japanese had a taste of sulphur in it which to say the least gave it a flavour but not to our liking! I can only assume that it was rice specially prepared for sowing and that the sulphur would prevent vermin from eating it out of the ground; as we were very, very, hungry we were not so fussy. On other occasions we were able in the bright sunlight to notice that the rice grains were not always uniform in size or colour and to our dismay we discovered that we were eating a mixture of rice and weevils, as one remarked at the time we were lucky in getting a meat ration!

By this time most of the POWs were about one half of their pre-1942 weight and were clothed only in a pair of tattered khaki shorts (if they still had them) or a kind of loincloth made from sheeting. Again if they were lucky they had a battered hat (I had acquired an Aussie one in Thailand)

and on our feet we had sandals made from rubber tree wood with a webbing strap across the toes, some of us of course went barefoot. The hunger pangs were always there day and night and in conversation between ourselves food was a major source of discussion. We dreamt of the favourite meal we would order on getting home, but on a practical note we would have been satisfied at any time, if then by magic, a slice of bread had appeared in front of us. Anything that would break the monotony of plain rice was tried, small snakes, snails and even cats or dogs if they could be enticed into the encampment through the wire. These items were simply tossed into the embers of a fire and sampled when they were well done. I personally had a try at the snails but was not impressed, possibly they weren't the French variety! I always reckoned that I kept myself really fit as a young man but now at times I was beginning to feel a great deal less than A1. I caught a mild dose of Dengue Fever which took a little time to throw off, and I suffered from mild beriberi in my legs, but there was no way I was going to report sick as I knew from experience if I did it, would be a long road back. As 1944 went by the guards at the airfield seemed to me to get even more surly, we of course did not get precise news of how the war was progressing and maybe neither did the ordinary Japanese soldier. We would have been heartened if we had known that in the second half of 1944 the Allies were making considerable progress. We learnt after the war that during this period we had begun to recapture Burma, the Americans were back in the Philippines but what would have saddened us would have been the news that POW deaths were occurring as a result of the Allied bombing of the railway in Burma. During my second period in Changi Gaol I made friends with a number of other POWs and it is with regret that when the war was over, and I was back in the UK I did not make an effort to get in touch with them but as I will explain later my life on returning home still contrived to be a little hectic. In addition to Nigel Carruthers whom I mentioned earlier there was Stan Evans who came from Chester, Ernie Kirtley who pre-war was a librarian in Durham, two members of the Singapore defence volunteers namely Norman Deroza and Laurie Van Der Stratten, also Phil Bernstein a member of the Australian Army who came from Melbourne. The comradeship with these friends helped greatly to get through the monotony and hopelessness of life at Changi and even on the darkest days helped us to raise a smile and a joke to make life bearable. As we moved into 1945 on quite a number of days I was moved on to a different work party in a hilly area of Singapore nearer to the town and it became obvious that the work was aimed at constructing defences for the island. This work proved to be quite dangerous but at least in a way it raised our spirits confirming that not all was well with the Japanese nation. On one of the early days in 1945 with no cloud in the sky it was early morning and suddenly we heard a steady droning sound, quite faint at first then gradually getting louder. We looked up and those of us who still had good eyesight peered into the glaring sunlight and saw about 18 silvery specks at an enormous height crossing over Singapore. It was obvious that the Japanese guards were quite agitated and the working day was brought to an end early and we were returned to our Camp. After the war I gathered that the planes we saw that day were flying fortresses of the American air force and in the months that followed in the spring of that year bombs were dropped in the dock area of Singapore. I was not aware of the explosions at that time, which was not surprising bearing in mind that in Changi we were about twenty miles from the docks. We gathered later from the grapevine that unfortunately several POWs had been killed whilst working there. Whether it was a direct result of the bombing or simply that the Japanese were becoming a little spiteful, the rations of rice per day got even less and by now nearly all POWs were weak and badly suffering from malnutrition – so much so that it became very difficult to raise the numbers for the work parties and of course the number of deaths mounted up. At this time in early 1945 we were being allowed to write the odd postcard home, and I have often thought that relatives receiving those cards would have anticipated that at the end of the war their son or husband was alive when in fact they had died in the last few months of the war.

The work of constructing tunnels and caves for the defence of Singapore was stepped up although work on the airfield still continued. The tunnels and caves were dug with hardly any shoring up with timber and I remember that on one party which I was a member, our faith was 100% in a POW from Durham (an ex miner) whose knowledge of mining so impressed the Japanese guard that in a short while he was quite happy to give him overall charge. When the Durham lad considered there was a possibility of a roof fall in a tunnel and called "everyone out!" the Japanese went off like a shot and won the race to the tunnel entrance by the literal mile! We were now in the spring of 1945 and of course rumours were rife in the camp at Changi. It would appear that matters were going splendidly against Germany but the trouble was, could we believe the rumours? From the attitude of the Japanese we felt that they were not doing so well either, again the thought of our eventual fate occupied our minds, at least it took our minds off food. About this time in the late spring of 1945 those POWs who were still working at the docks reported that there was feverish work there unloading stores, equipment and more importantly ammunition. To us this all pointed to priority being given to the defence of Malaya and Singapore and as it was also rumoured at that time that the war in Europe had ended, it was with trepidation we awaited the next few weeks. Always in our minds that even if there was the chance that the war was coming to an end, what would be the chances of our survival? If, it came at the end, down to hand to hand fighting what would be our fate? At present casualties continued to mount up, malnutrition was always there but malaria increased rapidly which meant that the number of POWs available for work were simply not available, and even the Japanese realised this and slightly lessened their demands. Bearing in mind that none of us had any protection from mosquitoes I could not understand why I personally never caught malaria, although all my friends around suffered from it from time to time. I can only presume that although subject to mosquito bites every day my blood in some way was repugnant to the buggers! Of course we did not know it at the time but the war was definitely drawing to a close; looking back at those last two months or so are now hazy to me but I have no doubt that the work on the defences was stepped up, and for me it was hard labour from dawn to dusk every day. On my return each day to my cell at Changi I would gobble up my rice and fall asleep immediately to be followed at the break of day by parading for another day's work.

This was a day after day routine so you can appreciate my astonishment when one day in about the middle of August after we were paraded had told there was no work that day and we were to return to our cell. This of course gave rise to great speculation, after all a holiday only came round on the Emperor's birthday! Further speculation developed when work was cancelled for a further two days following which we were given to understand that the war for the time being had stopped. What was even more peculiar was that the Japanese guards had become a little more polite and even the rations were slightly increased. Mark you some of us were sceptical, shall we say we smelled a rat, maybe we were being fattened for the slaughter! However these worries began to disappear especially when after a few more days Japanese guards simply disappeared and there seem to be quite a bit of air activity over Singapore. I remember that on one day soon after I was strolling outside the gaol I met a British paratrooper approaching me up the road. He was obviously English in that we exchanged greetings in the usual manner i.e. "good morning, it's a nice day". It was more than that; it was the greatest day of my life! As far as I can remember this episode occurred at the end of August and from there on matters proceeded reasonably swiftly, although of course not quick enough for us, we were only interested in getting home as soon as possible. You will appreciate that after 3 1/2 years of imprisonment which included our exploits on the railway, our wardrobes did not amount to much, in most cases something to cover our loins and if we were lucky a home-made pair of wooden sandals. Therefore to our delight, articles of clothing became available which turned out to be highly coloured T-shirts, linen shorts, and Japanese canvas boots with split big toes. What was more important, our food greatly improved and although it still mainly consisted of rice, the accompanying vegetable stew was a lot better. One or two newspaper and radio men arrived and our padre made a broadcast to London; the padre was the Rev Noel Duckworth who before the war, I believe in 1936, was the cox of the Cambridge boat race crew before becoming padre to the Cambridgeshire Regiment; after the war and sometime later he became a bishop in East Anglia. I did have a copy of his speech which I put into my scrapbook but as I will tell you later that scrapbook was deposited in the museum at the Bridge on the River Kwai when I visited it 65 years later.

A few days later Lady Mountbatten arrived at the prison with her staff and as that included some very pretty female members of the Armed Forces the visit was greatly appreciated by us, I think we had forgotten what females looked like. Mark you our strength needed a great deal more building up to fully show how pleased we were! On 12 September 1945 the Supreme Allied Commander South East Asia namely Lord Louis Mountbatten received the surrender of the Japanese forces in south-east Asia, who were under the command of General Itagaki. We now all knew for sure that the war was definitely over as for a brief period after the end of August it was rumoured that the Japanese surrender ordered by its Emperor was going to be disobeyed by the local Japanese commander. Of course by now we knew the full story leading up to the Japanese surrender, how the Japanese military forces in the last few months had their backs to the wall, all the territory in the Pacific had been recovered along with Burma. The final stage of the war would have been to invade Japan itself and there is no doubt that such an invasion would have been resisted 100% resulting in a colossal loss of life both military and civilian. In my opinion the news that the dropping of two atom bombs had prevented such an outcome of the war dragging on, was the only acceptable solution, and of course there is no doubt, from maybe selfish reasons, that action saved our lives. You must remember that for 3 1/2 years we had not received any authentic news, of course there were always rumours, some of which had a vestige of truth, so it was with great enthusiasm we asked questions what had happened in the world during that time. We now had the opportunity of sending a message home to confirm that we had survived and I know that my parents received the news in a cable sent via Colombo. I found out later that my old friend and workmate George Young with whom I'd lost touch early in the war had also survived, and as his parents and mine both lived in the same area of London they had kept in touch and relayed to each other any messages received. A few days after the surrender proceedings in Singapore Louis Mountbatten paid us a visit in Singapore prison, and of course now that our officers were now conducting matters, in shall we say, full regimental fashion, it was decided that he would be received on the Esplanade in front of the prison with a guard of honour. It was decided that this would consist of three squads of 30 men each from the British, Australian, and Dutch POWs, each squad to be lined up in three rows of 10 men. I suppose it was a typical example of military b******t to be carried out with some difficulty. After all reasonably fit men had to be found and it could hardly be said we were dressed uniformly bearing in mind the coloured T-shirts and variety of footwear . I took it as an honour to be picked for the British squad and in due course we were lined up when Mountbatten arrived. He and his entourage of staff officers were immaculate, their white suits crisp, buttons gleaming and medals glittering. On the order "open ranks" we shuffled to obey and the brass hats slowly carried out the inspection, Mountbatten pausing in front of the occasional man to make a comment. What he thought of it all I have no idea, it must have been the most nondescript, pathetic looking guard of honour ever to have been formed in British military history! However he graciously thanked the guard commander and made a rapid retreat to the Officer's Mess which by now would have been installed as a priority. There were Army photographers present on the occasion but as far as I can ascertain a picture of this guard of honour has never been published. I would have loved to have had a copy for my scrapbook but I could quite understand if the military authorities had decided it was best for such a photograph to be consigned to the scrapyard! By now the days of September were passing by and of course we were anxiously awaiting news regarding our departure for home. We had been free for over three weeks and although food had improved both in quantity and variety, it still had a mainly Asian content, and we longed for home plus the eggs and bacon! Time was passing too slowly, someone turned up and gave us a film show. I recall that it was a Bob Hope film which contained one incident causing a good laugh. At one stage in the film Bob played the part of a pirate, got his hook stuck in the door and when he was left without a hand blamed his loss on its the Japanese manufacturer. We also passed the time in the evenings playing cards, though not for money – we had none! One day I was given a pass to go into Singapore town (oh yes the Army was back into its regimental mood), a truck had appeared to take us for a two-hour stroll around the town. Singapore was still a little shambolic but the Chinese were rapidly recovering and getting things in order, so much so that I was able to get photographic copies of the Japanese surrender which I had taken a few days ago, later these will go into my scrapbook (now in the Kwai Museum). Then as supply ships arrived in the Singapore docks we were issued with Army tropical kit in a delightful shade of green together with the usual army boots which played havoc with our virgin feet which hadn't had a covering for a very long time.

Finally we received news of our proposed departure to the UK and I found myself as the senior fit artillery NCO in Changi prison preparing for it. I still have my notebook with the written instructions I received at the time from a Captain Sparke which read as follows. The 82 other ranks (from artillery regiments still remaining in Changi prison) are to be organised by myself into four lorry loads. The day of departure to be 28 September 1945, reveille at 0515, breakfast 0530, parade at the prison mortuary gate of 0600, filled water bottles to be carried. Without doubt we were fully back in the Army! It will give you some idea of what a mixed bag of Royal artillery men made up the party by my referring to my notebook and discovering 15 regiments were involved from anti-tank to field and anti-aircraft regiments. The largest number from an individual regiment was 21 from my own followed by 20 from the 125 anti-tank Regiment down to one from the seventh Coast Artillery Regiment. I checked them all onto the lorries and off we went to the docks where we were inspected and bade farewell to by one General M Dempsey following which we were introduced to our transport home namely the compact Polish troopship the MS Sobieski. The Sobieski had been taken over by the Admiralty way back in 1939 and was manned mainly by a Polish crew and it was obvious that it had been extensively engaged in all aspects of the war for six years. It was not a large ship being of 11,000 gross tonnage but was fairly modern with a good turn of speed and a plaque on the ship recorded a number of campaigns that it had been engaged in including landings in the Mediterranean and of course at D Day. During the war the Sobieski probably carried troops numbering well over 1000 but for its present job I believe the number of POWs to be carried was under 600 and therefore when we got on board, to our delight, we found that we had plenty of room. As I mentioned previously my responsibility was to get the artillery contingent on board and settled down into their bunks but I notice from my old notebook that I had listed the names of quite a lot of other POWs but now years later I cannot remember what my responsibility for them was. Most of them were obviously from the Royal engineers as they are recorded as Sappers but looking back one name now stands out, namely Sapper Ronald Searle. At any rate the Royal engineers' contingent followed us on board and I remember Searle, who at that time was still suffering from ulcerated legs, lying on the deck and enjoying the sun. At the time of writing this book (2012/13) it was with regret that I learned of Searle's death at his home in France at the beginning of 2012. Like me he had survived the Thai-Burma railway and had gone on to enjoy life for more than 65 years, with in his case fame and fortune as an artist, author and cartoonist. After a few hours the Sobieski with its cargo of "invalids" sailed away from Singapore with everyone vowing never to return and thanking the Almighty for our salvation, but of course 65 years later I did return, but that is another part of my story. The journey home was to last almost a month and I suppose that most people would think the time would be slow in passing, but for us it was like a holiday cruise, a good opportunity to build up our strength with sun, sea air and good food, what more could one ask for! The food was splendid – the menus full of variety with the most favoured item being the fresh baked bread with the morning's bacon and eggs, our dreams back at Changi had come true!

On the next day with the Sobieski heading up the Malacca Strait I was approached by the senior officer on board to organise a small detachment of reasonably fit men to help each day with getting stores up from the hold to the kitchens. This small task only took a couple of hours each day but it enabled me to strike up a very profitable friendship with the Polish storekeeper in that during the intense heat of the day he provided us with a never ending supply of iced drinks. In addition he was the source of a supply of duty-free cigarettes, the popular brands in sealed tins of 50, as of course in those days almost everyone smoked. So we proceeded on our journey clearing the north coast of Sumatra and then turning west across the Bay of Bengal on our way to Columbo where our ship was refuelled and restocked and at the same time allowing us a day ashore. Columbo of course had been an important place during the war against the Japanese, being a principal naval base, at first in a defensive role but later in a more aggressive one as the tide turned for the Allied forces in Burma. As we wandered through the town it was obvious that the townsfolk and the authorities were rapidly getting back to peacetime normality, now that the centre of military activity had moved eastwards to Singapore. I took the opportunity to find the office of my assurance company employer where I was entertained for a few hours and who kindly cabled the company's London office passing on a message from me to my parents. The journey home continued across the Indian Ocean into the Gulf of Aden and on into the Red Sea where the heat was intolerable but our kindly Polish storekeeper was most obliging in allowing our little party to sit in a refrigeration room with the door open, also supplying us with the necessary cold beverages. We then made it to Suez where at the military installation we received normal khaki UK kit to replace our jungle green, following which we proceeded through the Canal to Port Said. There the usual bartering with the locals in their bum boats took place before we turned into the Mediterranean, with me now the proud owner of a very smart leather suitcase, just the thing to hold the tins of Senior Service cigarettes! The journey through the Mediterranean was uneventful but extremely pleasant and in due course we stopped at Gibraltar presumably for refuelling and where we discarded our jungle green and put on our battledress for the winter. At the same time there was the opportunity to send a further message home. We turned into the Atlantic and headed northwards with all of us seething with anticipation as each mile went by and home waters came nearer. We could not bear to leave the deck as we sailed through St George's Channel and the Irish Sea as we tried to catch a glimpse of the UK coastline which we had not seen for four years.

Finally we entered the Mersey and anchored opposite the Liverpool Quays for a full day whilst we understood that negotiations had to be made with the dockworkers who were at that time on an unofficial strike. However I gathered that once they were aware that the Sobieski was carrying repatriated POWs all barriers were lowered and the ship was tied up to the Quay. Disembarkation followed early next morning which I believe was on 25 October 1945 and its organisation was first class with every POW having the assistance of a soldier to carry his kit ashore for him, for which I was extremely grateful bearing in mind my two kit bags, and also the leather suitcase carrying of course the cigarette hoard! However I did make a bad mistake in that when I took a fond farewell of the Polish storekeeper and was presented by him with two large beautiful pineapples as a gift, I foolishly forgot to pack them and left them behind! Days later when I mentioned this to my mother she could not have been more disturbed if I had left behind a couple of gold bars; of course this was understandable bearing in mind that folk at home in the war years had forgotten what a pineapple looked like. Once ashore we were bussed to the transit camp at Huyton where for the remainder of the day we were medically examined, our kit brought up to date with insignia of rank and regiment, issued with new documents and very importantly given an advance of pay. It was early reveille next morning and having been passed fit to go on leave it was off to Lime Street station for us who were London bound. It was a slow train and being October it was dark when we arrived at Euston station where we were split into groups according to which London district was our destination. The five of us bound for south-east London were shepherded by a lady from the women's voluntary services to a small car; how she squeezed five soldiers, seven or eight kit bags and my splendid suitcase into that car was a miracle! I was lucky in that she decided that she would drop me off first in Eltham but I found it difficult to give directions with my nose pressed firmly against the roof of the car, however I made it, back home at last! As I extricated myself from the car the W.V.S. lady rang the doorbell and my father not expecting a visitor so late at night slowly opened the door; as you might expect it was a very emotional reunion. My father and I talked later and he did say that it was a memorable night for him as two sons had gone away to war, my brother Fred to Normandy and on to Berlin, and me to Singapore and now back. My father and mother had had a trying time with the home damaged by bombing and my mother injured by blast but now one son was back, with the other to follow shortly. Thinking about it I've no doubt that there were many families who had an equally difficult time, many far worse than ours, especially if casualties had occurred but all I can do is to thank the Lord that we were all eventually at home together. Of course my first question was "where's mother"? To which my father replied that she was across the road visiting a neighbour. I shot across the road, knocked on the door and the neighbour on seeing me screamed "you're Jack's back" and of course it was another emotional reunion but this time with buckets of tears. Of course my priority was now to get in touch with Helen which I did first thing the next morning and managed to get a phone conversation with her at the RAF barracks in Catterick. After over four years her voice was just the same and bearing in mind that during that time we had only received one or two postcards from each other we had a great deal to talk about. The first action required Helen to apply for leave and we were hopeful that this would soon be forthcoming when we would meet in London for a few days and then go on to Peebles. Now the rest of our lives together would be before us. In the first day or two back home whilst awaiting news from Helen as to when we could meet, I contacted members of my mother's family but naturally the first person I wanted to see was my grandfather Tom Carr and my reunion with him was very emotional. He was now blind and it was a tearful reunion, bearing in mind the losses, as a father, he had suffered in the First World War. Three of his sons had failed to return, Tom Carr Jr (who had served as a regular in 1911 at the Khyber Pass fighting Afghans) and was killed in 1917 and buried in Turkey; one son killed in Flanders and another lost at sea when his destroyer was sunk in the Baltic. No wonder he was pleased at the return of his eldest grandson, sadly he had not long to live, the games of cribbage were a thing of the past.

# Post-war to Peebles

## 1947–1973: Marriage to Helen

To me the next chapter in my life story would be the most important as on my return my telephone conversation with Helen had indicated that all was well between us. However looking at the reality of the situation I had to take into account that we had been apart for over four years with really no communication. We would have to start our relationship all over again, were we the same people? Had either or both of us changed in some way, I certainly may have done both mentally and physical, but not in my love for her. For four years Helen had been in the R.A.F. doubtlessly striking up many friendships and had moved from being a teenager to a more mature woman. Was I expecting too much? It was with apprehension that I faced our meeting. Within a day or two a message came from Helen that she had been granted seven days compassionate leave and that she would catch a train to London that weekend, needless to say I was overjoyed. As yet I had not been officially demobbed and therefore had no civilian clothes that fitted me, I turned up in my uniform on the Saturday afternoon at King's Cross station to await Helen's arrival. Of course I was there in plenty of time, the train was not due until about five o'clock and you might say I was a bag of nerves, now was the time to see if the old magic was still there. I personally on my part had no doubts, but I was worried whether Helen felt the same, although I had some reassurance in the fact that she appeared to be unattached and had waited for me all those years. I stood by the platform barrier and in due course the train from the North steamed in, the carriage doors were flung back, and in my reckoning about 300 members of the women's auxiliary air force resplendent in their blue uniforms alighted, and streamed towards the barrier. Of course all the W.A.A.F.'S were mixed up with other passengers so that made it even more difficult as I looked for one special Corporal in blue! I need not have worried, we spotted each other simultaneously and with smiles and tears the corporal and the sergeant clung together in what is known nowadays as "the big clinch". Helen looked absolutely marvellous and as we chatted her soft Scottish border accent was music to my ears, that moment was probably the most happiest of my life. We went to the station tearoom and over a cup of tea we talked quite simply about everything, we covered the past the present and the future, we could have gone on talking for hours and so all doubts you could say went out of the window. So off to Eltham we went to spend a couple of days with my parents before going up to Scotland. In those days although we were engaged any what was then known as "hanky-panky" was not on and therefore Helen had my room and I settled for the box room, real love would have to wait until we were married, how frustrated could one get! Two days later we were off to Scotland; it was the morning train from Kings Cross to Edinburgh and in those years the trains were packed to overflowing and finding a seat was very difficult. However we squeezed into a compartment with the cooperation of fellow passengers, many other travellers having to stand in the corridor for the whole of the journey. Refreshments were not available so it required quick sorties at the main stops to station restaurants. This always gave rise to anxiety as to whether you made it back before the train steamed off again. Travelling in the years just after the war was not easy, it was definitely a time of austerity, a question of "that's what's available, take it or leave it", and that applied to food, clothing and accommodation as well. From Edinburgh it was an hour and a half on the bus to Peebles and Helen and I made our way wearily to her parent's house in Rosetta Road. They occupied the top flat and Helen's grandmother the bottom one so needless to say etiquette ruled that as regards sleeping accommodation it was upstairs for Helen and downstairs for Jack! The remainder of Helen's leave only amounted to four or five days but it was a wonderful time, although it was winter the days were crisp and dry and each day we went for walks in the lovely countryside around Peebles, especially along the banks of the Tweed. It was a time of really getting to know each other again; it took us back in time to those precious few days in my 1941 embarkation leave. In due course Helen returned to Catterick and I made my way back home, we had of course discussed the possibility of getting married in the very near future but a decision as to the date would of course depend on Helen's discharge from the R.A.F. In the meantime I needed to discuss with my old employer as to when and on what terms I would return to work, and, in addition, where were we going to live?

Nowadays (2013) the Army authorities do a tremendous amount for soldiers returning from harrowing experiences suffered in various theatres of war, but of course in 1945/46 there was a limit as to what could be done owing to the numbers involved. I had arrived back in Liverpool after four years in prisoner of war camps and after a quick medical I had been put on a train back to my home the next day. My next communication from the Army was a printed letter from the artillery depot at Woolwich to welcome me back, and to let me know that if I had any worries to get in touch, but in the meantime I was informed I was on the "Y list" until such time when I would receive "final instructions as to my disposal". In a few weeks my final discharge came through following which I was demobbed, as far as I can remember, at Wembley in London. I never did find out what was entailed being on the strength of the "Y list". I suppose I should have asked at the time when the dear Lieutenant-Colonel Hackett wrote me such a nice letter welcoming me home! My recollections of the demob at Wembley are rather vague but the impression still with me is that it was far from a serious matter, in other words a bit of "a hoot". It was in fact a procedure by which you gave up the trappings of military life i.e. your uniform and the bits and pieces that went with it, and took on civilian life i.e. a suit and its accessories and at the same time receiving some clothing coupons. Most of the stuff was thrown at you in the usual Army manner, except for the suit, where apart from the size you had a choice, grey with chalk stripe or navy with chalk stripe, so with several hundreds of men I chose the grey which I felt was a more refined colour! The cut of the suit was not exactly Savile Row, in fact it was hardly "50 Shilling Tailors", but it was a reasonable swap for the battledress. For the benefit of people of the present-day the "50 Shilling Tailors" were well-known men's shops catering for the working class in pre-war years. However with a bank balance now quite healthy with Army back pay, plus the necessary clothing coupons, I made my way to London's Burlington Arcade (where providing you had the money and coupons, goods other than utility were available). I purchased a splendid sports jacket in a dogs tooth check plus light grey flannel trousers. I couldn't wait a moment to get adorned with my new purchases, Jack the Lad was now ready for all and sundry! By now I had agreed with the Australian life assurance company that I would return to work in the middle of February. Since the beginning of the New Year they had asked me to return as soon as possible owing to shortage of staff. I had also learned that Helen would probably get her discharge from the RAF in late March, which would lead to our getting married in April. There remained a problem of where we would live after our marriage but this was solved on a temporary basis by my parents offering us a room until my brother Fred was discharged from the Army. In modern parlance it was now "all systems go"!

Therefore on a Monday morning I turned up at the office in Cheapside resplendent in my demob suit, the "Burlington Arcade outfit" being deemed unsuitable for an office in the city and started work again as the Cashier's assistant at a salary of £325 per annum. I really enjoyed this job, just the two of us, the cashier being an elderly man on the point of retirement who travelled up to the city every day from Hastings on the coast. We had a little alcove on the front desk in constant touch with the general public, with a splendid view straight down Cheapside towards the Mansion House, also the work was far more pleasant than my previous job in the accounts department. Dealing with callers over the counter made work very interesting, we often dealt with notable people, including stage people. I remember on one occasion been entertained by Elsie and Doris Waters, two well-known comediennes of that era. Otherwise there was little change in my day to day office life, most of my pre-war colleagues had returned after the war with the exception of Howard who was still to be demobbed. My colleague George had of course been discharged at the same time as myself and on finding, surprisingly, Joe Lyons still operating, we again sampled at lunchtime, the famous pie and chips which we felt were not quite up to pre-war standard.

In due course Helen received her discharge and our wedding was arranged to take place on 27 April 1946 at the Waverley Hotel in Peebles. My parents travelled up to Scotland with a certain amount of trepidation for the wedding but despite a little language difficulty everything took place splendidly. The reception was held in the Waverley Hotel, a whip round for food coupons had ensured a fine meal with a wedding cake. Unfortunately the hotel (owned by a Scottish relation, therefore free) was unlicensed, much to everyone's dismay especially the Minister who conducted the service! As Dr Beeching had yet to appear on the scene, Helen and I were able to depart on our honeymoon by rail from Peebles, and were seen off by the whole of the wedding party, all Scots, except my mother and father. I felt I was leaving them to fend for themselves in a foreign land! And so to Edinburgh for an overnight hotel stop before taking the train via London to our honeymoon destination in Bexhill-on-Sea on the south coast. The hotel in Edinburgh somehow didn't seem very romantic, and in any case we were very shy (young people believe it or not were like that in those days), so we decided we would go to the variety show then on at the Empire Theatre and have a good laugh! If I remember rightly top of the bill was "Nat Mills and Bobby". The next day we arrived at the small hotel in Bexhill and I'm pleased to say we had extremely good weather and a romantic and passionate holiday. Whilst at the hotel we tried to appear nonchalant, just an ordinary couple enjoying an early holiday but we didn't fool anyone, especially when we turned up for the evening meal not knowing that during the afternoon there had been the most violent thunderstorm there had been for years! After the honeymoon it was back to "old clothes and porridge", as they say in Scotland, with me setting out on the next Monday morning for work in the City leaving Helen at home to her own devices.

Our immediate object was to get our own house. Morning papers and estate agents lists were scoured and any possible lead was followed up either by phone, post, or even calling at an address in the early hours of the morning. I had been promised a mortgage by my employer subject to my depositing 25% of the purchase price of any property, and therefore I was in the market for a semi-detached house in south-east London in the region of £1200. At the beginning of 1946 it was a hopeless task, houses were like gold dust, and comparatively speaking rents were high. As we went through the remainder of 1946 the "living in one room" syndrome plus not having very much to do by herself during the day made it difficult for Helen to settle down and of course she missed Scotland. By this time my old colleague Howard Agar had returned to the office and his Irish wife Meta was good enough to find Helen a job beside her in the publication offices of "The Spectator" situated just off Waterloo Bridge, and this gave her added interest to her day. Until we could get our own house we thought it best not to consider starting a family but all our endeavours to get our own accommodation were fruitless which for all young couples then was very disheartening Today in 2013 that is precisely the situation for many young people. Apart from the house hunting we enjoyed the summer and autumn of 1946, particularly at weekends when at every opportunity we would explore the Kent countryside. Remember rationing was still in force and we still worked on a Saturday morning, the five-day week being a long way off. During the year, from my advantage point in the office, I remember Lord Mountbatten going in procession to the Guildhall, probably to be granted the freedom of the city of London. It was a splendid affair, he was in full dress uniform and was escorted by the household cavalry, and for me it brought back the poignant memory of that guard of honour outside Changi prison. At that time in 1946 as Viceroy of India he was actively engaged in the transition of that country to independence and history has recorded the turbulence that this caused, with the eventual establishment of the separate state of Pakistan. During the year we went on holiday back to Peebles, which we enjoyed immensely, but looking back I think it only made Helen very homesick and I began to doubt very much whether she would ever settle down as a housewife in London. Christmas and New Year came and went, following which my parents received the news that my brother Fred, who was still stationed in Berlin, had married a young Church of Scotland worker called Sheena MacLachlan from Strachur in Scotland. Now he was likely to be demobbed in the early spring, which would mean that Helen and I would need to find alternative accommodation as my mother considered his need was greater than mine.

We would now have to redouble our efforts to either purchase or rent a house and in view of the shortage of property in London this was worrying. However out of the blue came a solution which required serious consideration. It was towards the end of January that Helen received the sad news that her grandmother had died and naturally Helen made the trip up to Peebles for the funeral. A few days after her return she mentioned that the upstairs flat that her parents had been living in was now vacant, as they had taken over the grandmother's house below. If we wanted the empty flat it was there for the taking. Naturally, accommodation being our chief worry, Helen and I discussed the possibility of moving to Scotland but the first problem to solve was that of employment. Accordingly I explored the possibility that my current employer could offer me something in the nearest city, that being Edinburgh. However, with regret the manager could not oblige, so the next move was to find out whether a position could be found in another company. I wrote similar letters to the principal assurance companies in Edinburgh namely the "Standard Life" and the "Scottish Widows". People who work in the city of London normally have no worries about the distances they have to travel to their work, travel in south-east England is easy, weather is reasonable and many travel twenty or thirty miles or even more. So the fact that Peebles was almost thirty miles from Edinburgh city centre had no worries for me but I was soon to find out that the weather in the Scottish Borders could prove unpredictable. I soon had answers to my letters; the "Scottish Widows" informed me there was no vacancy and that my letter was on file, the "Standard Life" was happy to give me a job subject to an interview at their London office and a satisfactory medical examination. Having been a recent Japanese prisoner of war I was slightly worried about the medical but that was passed without a hitch. At the interview it was agreed that I would commence my duties in Edinburgh on the first Monday in March 1947 at the same salary I was receiving from my present employer, namely £325 per annum. I handed my notice in about the middle of February and at that time Howard and Meta Agar were extremely helpful and looked after us for a week before we made our journey to the North. Our belongings were few, a bed and some odds and ends which were put into a railway container which was not delivered until almost a month later. This was due to one of the worst winters on record, the whole country was in the grip of ice and snow, power stations ran short of coal and the government decreed that that all rail transport was to concentrate on the delivery of fuel. Accordingly our miserable belongings were shunted into a siding, I believe at Newcastle, and forgotten about. Helen and I spent the first few weeks in Peebles with a mattress on the floor! Worse was to follow. It had snowed in London before we left, and had not stopped on the journey and on arrival in Peebles it was still snowing, with about over a foot of snow covering the ground. This resulted in all transport to and from and in Scotland being either delayed or cancelled; I was beginning to think that I had been rather foolhardy in ever contemplating the move. Helen and I had a week to get ourselves shipshape, we had a mattress, we borrowed utensils that we needed and had a little fuel for the fire; however we had our love to keep us warm!

On my first week with my new company I only managed to get into Edinburgh on three days out of six, and on those three days I was late owing to the train getting stuck in the snow and having to be rescued by snow ploughs. I really did now begin to have doubts as to whether my move had been a wise one. I expected at the end of the week to be informed that the Standard Life considered my attendance record to be unsatisfactory and accordingly be given the old Heave ho! I'm pleased to say that they were most understanding and they and myself proceeded to have a very happy relationship until my retirement at the end of 1980. Apart from my attendance record in that first week, Helen and I unfortunately had our first disagreement, over the Scottish pastime of golf! Monday was one of the days I reached Edinburgh just after 10 a.m., met the Secretary Mr A. R. Reid, followed by another official, then to my new department to meet its head, a Robert Macdonald. Everyone was extremely courteous though it seemed that they found it a little difficult to understand my phraseology, this was perhaps understandable as basically I was a cockney who had yet to learn the Scottish language. Robert Macdonald gave me some departmental instructions to read and after a few minutes came over for a chat during which he gave me some very important advice, "Jack" he said, "if you want to get on in the Standard you will need to play golf," to which I replied I would bear that in mind. After another 20 mins or so he came back to let me know that, "it so happens I have three clubs I could sell to you for a pound each and I am willing to throw in an old putter". At that time I had no knowledge of golf, cricket was my game, but in order to foster relations I agreed to the transaction. Trouble with Helen occurred later when in darkness, trudging home through two feet of snow, she met me at the door and enquired as to what I had under my arm. On being informed that I had spent about half a week's wage on three rather worn golf clubs she let me know in no uncertain terms (in Border dialect) that I had wasted money, also bearing in mind the existing weather conditions it was unlikely I would see a golf course until about May. At a later time when I related the incidence to a colleague he simply remarked that Robert McDonald came from Balquidder, the same area frequented by

Rob Roy MacGregor who was also a bandit! However I would like to place on record that I did learn to play golf by making adjustments to my cricket strokes, and that Robert Macdonald was quite correct in saying that playing golf was an asset in the Standard Life assurance company. In Scotland being a member of a golf club has the same standing as being a member of a Masonic lodge!

The general manager of the company at that time was Andrew Davidson, a charming man who prided himself on remembering the name of each member of his staff, and to keep himself up to date, he visited every department on a regular basis. At that time practically all the staff, probably less than 100, worked in the single building at 3, George Street, Edinburgh. I should mention that I had been placed in the Policy Department which dealt with the assurance policy documents and all matters pertaining to them. This came as a surprise to me bearing in mind my previous work experience in accounts and cash departments, but with staff still to return from the forces I guess I was put where I was needed. Andrew Davison on spotting me as a newcomer extracted the information that I lived in Peebles and as he was a keen fisherman he immediately assumed that anyone living by the Tweed would likewise be engaged in that sport. On later visits to the department he would take it for granted that I had profound knowledge on the subject, which was rather one-sided, with me agreeing to all his observations. I later learned that he had the let of a stretch of a river in the North for salmon fishing and for a long time I was fearful that he would invite me (as an expert?) to join him for a weekend fishing! I should've come clean when he first came into the department but as a young newcomer confronted by a Scottish general manager, I was at a loss for words and was much happier when Andrew Davidson retired after a few years. Why are the Scots so obsessed with sports such as golf, fishing and even curling and appear to ignore cricket! I really enjoyed my work in the department having a good rapport with my Scottish colleagues, especially the departmental head, good old MacDonald, who even invited me one Saturday afternoon to Murrayfield to see Scotland in a rugby union game. My first connection with the game since being ordered to play against the Irish Guards seven years ago. Robert even took me home to meet his wife, who provided the marvellous Scottish high tea! My work in the office mainly consisted initially of drafting life assurance policies to be typed by experienced typists, and after time I progressed to checking the policies before they went for signature by an official and a company director. My main interest outdoors was in football, a team was formed within the company, and for a year or so I played an active part. I would like to think that the profile of the team was raised by my inclusion, but I doubt it. At the same time I endeavoured to pick up and put into practice the rudiments of golf as I still had in mind the advice I had been given. Helen also managed to get herself a part-time job and since we were only paying a nominal rent for the flat we had no monetary worries, which enabled us now to seriously think about having children. Unfortunately all our efforts in this direction were not rewarded; in those days advisory clinics were very few in the UK. However about three years passed by and to our joy Helen became pregnant. Unfortunately our happiness was blown away when Helen lost the baby girl at about six months, and to this day I still recall the misery we both felt at the time. In those days fertility clinics generally were not available. If children did not come along then it was regarded as hard luck, mark you we did feel we had received our fair share of that. However we both got on with life together and if anything it made our love for each other even deeper. In due course our lives moved into the early 1950s when news coverage was mainly about the Cold War, espionage and defections, with the possibility of conflict between the West and Russia. Accordingly The Standard Life purchased Kings Meadows house and grounds on the outskirts of Peebles for the storage of important records. These were the days before records could be kept on microfiche etc, and it was also considered prudent to organise accommodation, which might be necessary for a skeleton staff to operate from Peebles. At that time I was the only member of staff living in Peebles, so it was arranged by the deputy general manager A.E. Bromfield that Helen and I would take up residence in Kings Meadows as caretakers, although I personally would still continue to work in Edinburgh.

About a year prior to Helen and I moving to Kings Meadows house I had stopped playing football as my interest in learning to play golf increased, even though football was to take up quite a bit of my spare time. My father-in-law was on the committee running the local football team, Peebles Rovers, who were members of the East of Scotland league and as he felt he had done a long enough stint he proposed that I should take his place. Within a season or two I became the secretary of it following a decision to run the club with a semi-professional team, and this took up a greater percentage of my spare time. As soon as the Scottish football season ended clubs in the various professional leagues issued lists of players not being retained, and what was more important to us, those players were being let go without a fee. These lists were scanned, addresses and phone numbers obtained and it was my job to get in touch with any player likely to be interested in joining a non-league club in the following season. Such players were normally coming to the end of their playing careers with their main interest being able to continue playing. The team therefore consisted mainly of professional players from outside Peebles plus one or two local amateurs and I spent a great deal of time travelling to see players and invite them to trial matches. I remember on one occasion signing a professional named Burgess who was paired up with a local player named Maclean. In the first league match it could be said that this was not a success and I was advised in rather a raucous manner "for God's sake send them back to Russia". It was of course the time of the Cold War with its defections and these two names were plastered over every newspaper in the country! Like all clubs finance was always a problem, outside sponsorship was always needed, and I was required to approach local shops and gentry for support, and I must say that writing from my new address of Kings Meadows House did help. (It's a coincidence that this year 2013 the house is up for sale for about £2 million). In the 1950s a major Edinburgh club, Hibernian were enjoying success with several of the players representing Scotland, one can call to mind such players as Younger, Johnstone, Smith, Reilly, Turnbull and Ormond with the club having a very proficient chairman in Harry Swan together with a top-class manager, Hugh Shaw. The club had an efficient method of bringing on their own young players and to this end they ran a third team in the East of Scotland league, but with a surplus of youngsters they could not always give every player a game. Our chairman John Brown represented the East of Scotland on the Scottish football Association committee and so had a friendship with Harry Swan. They accordingly arranged that two Hibernian players would be transferred to Peebles on a loan basis (it may well be the first instance of the loan system in Scottish football). Accordingly on one of my lunch breaks in Edinburgh I made my way down to Easter Road to complete the necessary papers. I did this in the presence of Harry Swan and Hugh Shaw in the boardroom and as usual with football transactions it was a very hospitable occasion cemented with the very best single malt, served in a half pint tumbler! I left Easter Road and made my unsteady way up Leith Walk back to the office to face my usual task of checking a number of assurance policies, luckily with some degree of success! The influx of experienced professional players from 1952 onwards produced an excellent record for Peebles Rovers in qualifying in the next decade for the Scottish Cup. In fact on two occasions they won the Qualifying Cup and during that time met several well-known Scottish league teams. In addition they made several sorties north to play Highland clubs, with success against Inverness Thistle and Ross County. A game worthy of note was a Scottish cup saga against Brechin City which took three games to settle and including extra time lasted for 420 mins of play, this may well be a Scottish record! After these glory years, things went rapidly downhill, with better transport and more car owners, supporters moving to the Premier division teams in Edinburgh and after a brief spell in Scottish junior football the local team reverted to the amateur status. I personally had no interest in junior football and so resigned, in any case I was spending a great deal of time on the golf course. Looking back I suppose I rather neglected my dear Helen, if only at weekends, but I like to believe she was pleased that as an Englishman I had successfully integrated myself into the community and appeared to have been accepted by all my Scottish friends. Helen and I missed not having children but with regard to this aspect of our life together we were helped a great deal by having the children of her sister Margaret almost every school holiday to stay with us. Kenneth, Andrew and Isabel on their visits gave us a great deal of pleasure, especially as in a way we could be a part of their growing up, and later Kenneth joined the Standard Life and stayed with us until he moved to Edinburgh. So the years went by, Helen had one or two part-time jobs, one of which was as an assistant librarian in Peebles, which gave her a great deal of pleasure as of course when I met her the first time way back in 1940, she worked in the newsagents and booksellers shop. Despite my peculiar golf action I did improve at the game so much so that I succeeded in winning a couple of the Company's competitions, the principal one being for the individual knockout competition on handicap. The venerable trophy at stake was in the form of a silver putter, which over the decades had been won by a line of venerable Scotsmen, with probably the early ones now turning in their graves with the trophy having been won by a Sassenach from Camberwell! In the early 1960s, peaceful Peebles was disturbed by politicians on the occasion of the 1965 by-election, which was covering the new constituency of Tweeddale, Ettrick, and Lauderdale. There appeared on the scene a very likeable young man, not long out of university, who stood for the Liberal party. He seemed to radiate new ideas coupled with a pleasing personality, and his name was of course David Steel, who later became the first speaker in the newly formed Scottish Assembly. He was elected with a sizeable majority and the next evening he made a memorable speech on the steps of the Tontine hotel, in front of a cheering crowd including Helen and I.

As we approached our third year in Kings Meadows house, Helen and I felt that we would like our own house in Peebles and in due course purchased "Gympie", a small stone built house in St Andrews Road, where we were to spend almost 20 happy years. The house had been built before the turn of the century by one "Hammy Neilson" who had returned to Peebles after several years as a gold miner near the town of Gympie in Australia. Needless to say, on discovering the history of the house, I did make a search of the attic for any mislaid gold nuggets! The years rolled by, and Helen and I were happy to share together the pleasant times that followed. I had progressed in the Standard Life and Helen was living as a normal housewife. We of course had lots of friends, our evenings were full, and with the weekends free, we were able, in our car, to explore Scotland even as far as John O'Groats, it was a happy time and my love for Helen and Scotland knew few bounds. We celebrated our 25th wedding anniversary in 1971 with a dinner dance for our friends at a hotel near Biggar. So that we could all enjoy the evening without any restrictions or limitations the party was transported from Peebles in the well-known local coach called the "Beltane Queen" and a belting time was had by all! You can imagine, therefore, the surprise we felt when, three years later, we found ourselves bound for Birmingham, England. We were going to be faced with making a decision which would alter our lives forever; for my part, in later years I found it hard to justify the decision I made then in 1973. Prior to that year the Standard Life's Policy Department had gone through a change, with the advent of the computer age, the actual policy documents were no longer typed but produced mechanically. Accordingly a new section was setup to deal with this and a colleague, Sandy Purvis, was placed in charge. The remainder of the department left, dealt with servicing only existing policies and by that time yours truly was in charge. Thus Sandy and I were more or less in a similar position contemplating what lay ahead for either of us, 1973 would prove to be a momentous year for both of us.

# Then on to Birmingham

## 1973–1978: Helen's death, eventual marriage to Joyce

By the time that Helen reached the age of fifty she suffered one or two health problems, the main one being rheumatoid arthritis, which, as the years went by increased in its severity, but at first the discomfort was held in check by prescribed drugs. This problem was one amongst others that had to be considered when, towards the end of 1973, I was encouraged by the company to apply for the post of regional office manager in Manchester. At that time, the Standard Life was pursuing a policy of moving work (in connection with the production of assurance policies) out of Edinburgh to regional offices. At the time I had reached a reasonable clerical grade, life was comfortable, and living in Peebles meant a lot to Helen and I. However, if given the post, it would have resulted in promotion, and signalled that I was not averse to moving on, even at the age of fifty-three. One other point that Helen was aware of was that she had a favourite cousin living at Alderley Edge, near Manchester, so obviously she would have a friend nearby. We agreed I should apply and I soon found that Sandy Purvis and I were the only candidates on the shortlist. In due course we both attended interviews in Manchester following which I was given to understand that Sandy had been chosen, the deciding factor being my age. I must say this made me feel somewhat old but Helen and I were not duly perturbed at losing. Within a week or two a second regional post arose, this time in Birmingham but I promptly gave this a miss. For one thing we knew no one in Birmingham and secondly the area did not appeal, also having been passed by for Manchester I did not relish a second rejection. However the next day I was asked by the Agency Manager, who was responsible for the post being filled, why I had not applied, to which I gave the reasons afore mentioned, upon which he made it clear he wanted me to take the post. Again, Helen and I discussed the matter fully, finally agreeing to go to Birmingham, knowing there was the distinct possibility that I could retire at the age of sixty, thus allowing a move back to Peebles six years later. We still had a problem of Helen's health, but with the excellent medical facilities in Birmingham we felt sure she would receive first-class treatment for the rheumatoid arthritis.

Therefore in the autumn of 1973 as Regional Office Manager for the Midlands, I met, in Birmingham, the new Regional Manager, Eddie Wedgewood, who like myself had served in the Royal Artillery during the war, and needless to say we got on like a house on fire. The Regional Office (installed in a palatial new building) had to be set up with clerical staff of about 100 in number – additionally I had to find a house so that Helen could join me as soon as possible. The staff situation was eased by using members from the old Birmingham office in the city centre but we still had a number (about 80) to find and this was accomplished in due course with a few problems on the way. The office had been equipped with visual display units (a new innovation in those days) linked by line to Edinburgh for rapid transmission of business and so it was necessary to find staff adept at using keyboards; in addition clerical staff, secretaries and typists were also required. This was achieved in a remarkably short time, though looking back I think I engaged quite a number of ladies who were very proficient but perhaps a little older than required by the Edinburgh head office. It was pointed out to me by the company's finance officer that as salaries tended to be based on age, would I please remember it was a case of " the younger the better"! However, needs must! During this time being in a hotel, I was also searching for a house which I found in Solihull, a district I was assured was a must for anyone moving to work in Birmingham. The house required central heating and as this was a number one requirement for Helen in view of the rheumatoid arthritis, this was installed just before Christmas and Helen moved down shortly after. Although I had gone back on one or two weekends to Peebles, I had been away for almost three months and I was overjoyed as if we were getting back together again on return from the Army! Helen and I quickly settled down in 47, Kingslea Road, Solihull, and we soon got to know our neighbours who were extremely pleasant and friendly.

In particular were our next door neighbours May and Barry Homer who were to play an important part in my life in the years to come. The staff in the Regional Office settled down well and with the help of excellent colleagues I really did enjoy the work, and after a time, was able at weekends, to explore the surrounding countryside of Warwickshire. The garden of the house was of a reasonable size to enable me, with the help of a greenhouse, to produce fruit and vegetables; this pastime I really did enjoy and I became a very enthusiastic gardener. I would mention that at this time in 1974 my mother was living in a small cottage on the outskirts of Wells in

Somerset, my father having died in 1976 from lung cancer, so we found it easier to visit her than we did from Scotland. My mother and father had gone to Wells following my brother, who had taken up a position as a gardener (with the perk of the lodge cottage) on a large estate on the outskirts of the town. Unfortunately my brother was always looking for pastures new and after a year or two he decided to move to Cockermouth in Cumbria, thus leaving my parents (to my mind) more than a little in the lurch. About this time I received news that Sandy Purvis's wife had unfortunately died and that consequently he had applied to return to Edinburgh, a wish that had been granted. It would seem that the post of regional office manager might have a curse, how true. As I mentioned previously, the Regional Manager Eddie Wedgewood and I being of the same age and both having served in the armed forces during the war, worked really well together. This friendship continued outside office hours with Eddie and his wife and Helen and I sharing many a pleasant evening. Unfortunately, they had an autistic son who needed a great deal of care, and bearing in mind the responsibility of his job in a large company Eddie and his wife coped extremely well, always giving the boy all the love in the world.

The next few years went by and in the main Helen and I were extremely happy although of course when holidays came around, off we went back to our old stamping ground in Peebles and it was still our intention to return there for good on my eventual retirement in 1980. However, the rheumatoid arthritis was still giving Helen a great deal of trouble, as time went by life became extremely painful for her and several different forms of medication were prescribed by the consultants at Solihull Hospital. Several new drugs were prescribed to no avail, in fact, thinking back, the new American drugs probably caused her to lose weight and energy. By the time 1977 came around I was getting really worried about her health especially as during that year she had to spend a short time in hospital. Eventually, at the beginning of 1978, with her health deteriorating she was again taken back into hospital, where she suddenly died on 25 February 1978. I shall never forget that day; I had received a phone call at 7 a.m. on that Saturday to come at once to the hospital as the medical staff were concerned, and I was to be at Helen's bedside until she slipped away at about 8 p.m. During all of that day she did not recover consciousness, and never in the 93 years of my life would I want to ever suffer the grief I felt then. I went back to the house and was unable to get to sleep until the early hours of the morning, my mind constantly full of the same thought "why now and here away from Peebles?" Over and over in my mind I kept asking myself why did I take the job here and bring Helen away from the place she cared for?, obviously we were no longer going back together. Before I dropped off to sleep, I made up my mind that arrangements would have to be made to take her back to where she was born, to be amongst her family in the place she loved. A neighbour, Mr Mason, was very helpful in taking me to Sutton Coldfield to make special arrangements necessary for the coffin to be moved to Scotland and thence to burial in Peebles. At this time Helen's sister and family and all our friends both in Solihull and Scotland had been deeply shocked and of course all my colleagues who had known Helen missed her charm and Scottish accent.

Eventually I got up to Peebles for the family funeral and the graveside service which was conducted by the church of Scotland minister attached to the Leckie Memorial Church. I was amazed at the number of people that attended. Townsfolk who had known Helen from her school days and colleagues of almost five years ago from the company's head office in Edinburgh. Helen had always been a member of the Church of Scotland and of course after our marriage by the Minister of St Andrews Church I also joined that denomination; however during our short time together in Solihull we joined the local United reformed Church. It was very kind of the Minister at that church to conduct a service of remembrance which enabled colleagues and neighbours in the Midlands to attend. On my return to the Regional Office the loss of Helen made it difficult for me to concentrate on the day-to-day work and I did initially make an attempt to return to the Head Office of the company in Edinburgh. I did so because of my wish to get back to Peebles but my application was turned down, the reason being given that whereas Sandy Purvis was a younger man, I had a short time to go to my retirement and it was understandable that I should see the time out. When holidays came round in the summer I needed to get back up to Scotland to see all my friends. I decided to spend a day or two at the Open Championship at St Andrews and I was invited to join Helen's sister and all the family for dinner on the last day of the championship at Rufflets Hotel in St Andrews. I believe it was the last occasion that Jack Niklaus won the old claret jug and it was with great pleasure that we found he was staying at the hotel. Later in the evening he and his charming family paraded the cup and allowed us to take photographs. Some years previously I had watched Arnold Palmer also at St Andrews who quite happily gave me his autograph and you will gather by now that I had become a golfing enthusiast and I must say I've always found top golfers very approachable and very affable.

The rest of 1978 went by with me resigning myself to my job and of course at Christmas and New Year I went to Scotland again as I could not bear to be alone in the house at a time when for others it was a jolly and festive season. I had to be with people I knew, in surroundings which with Helen, I had loved in the past. I had come to the end of that fateful and in the main a very painful year. When I returned to the house there was of course a small heap of mail and amongst it was a letter from a lady called Joyce Homer, who I remembered was the sister of Barry Homer, my next door neighbour. It was a kind and charming letter expressing her sympathy for my loss and saying that on the one or two occasions she had met Helen she had enjoyed chatting to her. The letter jogged my memory and I recalled that during the summer before I went up to see the Open Championship, I had met Joyce on one occasion when she had paid her brother a visit, and we had a pleasant conversation over the garden fence. My memory of Joyce was that she was a lady a few years younger than myself who had been a widow for many years. Some weeks later feeling somewhat low in spirit and quite frankly needing companionship, I phoned her on the number she had left on her letter. It turned out to be the office number of the company she worked for as a receptionist, namely "Webley and Scott", one of the principal gun manufacturers in Birmingham. The conversation turned out to be the first of a number we had in the following weeks and eventually I suggested that we should meet up and possibly have a meal together, after all I thought, we are friends with no ties, therefore why not? About this time there was trouble in the world regarding oil supplies which led to a shortage of petrol in England, causing motorists to queue at petrol stations whenever overdue deliveries were made. Accordingly when Joyce and I made arrangements to meet one Sunday, to save petrol, she came down to Solihull from Birmingham city centre by train. After meeting her at Solihull station we went for a walk in the local park, it being a lovely bright day for that time of year. I thought I would take her for a nice meal in the early evening but being a Sunday the only suitable restaurant I could find was in Henley in Arden. Including that journey and taking Joyce back to Birmingham later on, needless to say, required a fair amount of my precious petrol! On reaching the Italian restaurant in Henley we found we were the only diners and as such received the attention of two or three waiters. On a cold Sunday night at that time of the year it was obvious that, since we were both wearing wedding rings, this was very much a suspicious liaison. A married couple would never have come out of their house in such weather! By now it was approximately one year since Helen's death and for me it had been a miserable and lonely time. If only I had been able to return to Scotland immediately at that time (to work in Edinburgh and live in Peebles) then I might have been able, with the help of friends, to carry on with life as a widower. Joyce was a vivacious and attractive woman and so our first meeting was followed by more during which we got to know each other, and found that we had a lot in common. In life I always found it difficult to live alone, I need company and Joyce was there.

At first we kept these meetings to ourselves, in fact we met in my house on one or two occasions without Joyce's brother next door being aware. It was still in my mind to return to Scotland in 1980 when I hoped to retire and naturally I sounded out Joyce's thoughts regarding living north of the border, but in no certain manner she made it clear that the possibility of going there, was to her, as unnerving as moving to the North Pole! By March our relationship was very close and I felt that it would be a wrench to part and for me to leave and make the eventual lone journey back to Scotland. Not only we talked the matter over several times and eventually we both made the mutual decision to marry and for the time being live in Solihull. We were married in Solihull register office on 18 April 1979 without telling anyone except for an office colleague and his wife who came along to be witnesses. In fact I went into work on the morning of the marriage, and being the office manager, arranged matters so that my colleague and I could leave in plenty of time for the ceremony taking place in the mid-afternoon. The marriage was by special licence which I had arranged previously and following the short ceremony Joyce and I had one or two photographs taken at a local studio and then returned to my house for a few hours before a celebratory dinner at a local restaurant. We arrived back at the house about 4.30 p.m., popped next door to give the news to Joyce's brother, surprising him and his family, but then were surprised ourselves by my nephew Kenneth (from Scotland) arriving unannounced at the door to pay a visit, being on a business trip in the area. As far as I can remember he may have joined us for our celebratory meal but no further! The following day was spent informing friends and relatives of our marriage, and in particular sending a telegram to my mother in Wells; we had of course phoned Joyce's mother the previous evening. Following my father's death in 1969 my mother had continued to live alone in her cottage but following a deterioration in her health it had become necessary for her to move into a nursing home in Wells. Helen and I had visited her from time to time from Solihull so I assured her over the phone, that I would come down with Joyce and see her as soon as possible. Joyce and I had decided that for the time being we would delay the honeymoon, so both of us were back at work within a day or so. When Joyce reported back to Webley and Scott where she had been receptionist for many years, the management and staff overwhelmed her with congratulations and best wishes for her future. In my case I think my colleagues were a little bit surprised and shocked!

After a while we found it expedient for Joyce to give up her job, as getting her from Solihull to Handsworth and back every working day in the Birmingham traffic was a difficult and time consuming job. We now gave thought to our honeymoon and decided to go to Jersey, in July for two weeks; we definitely felt the need for it! In a way it was not easy for Joyce to give up her job; as receptionist at Webley and Scott, the work was extremely interesting in that many notable persons came through the door to arrange for the purchasing of sporting guns and rifles. If these were not actually made by Webley and Scott, they were the gateway to other Birmingham gun makers who specialised in shot guns. The potential buyers, included of course, the landed gentry along with well-known sportsman; amongst the latter on one occasion, was Mr Kevin Keegan who in a charming conversation with Joyce was asked by her "and what do you do for a living?" Obviously Joyce did not follow the game! I remember learning from Joyce that customers requiring top-class shot guns needed to be measured and fitted for their gun. Of course Joyce had the charm which was necessary for such a job and I suppose it was one of the many things about her which led to my downfall! Although I knew that Joyce had been a widow for a good number of years and that her first husband had been a flight Sgt in the RAF during the war I was interested in knowing more about her family ties. Joyce had married William Ratcliffe in 1943 when they were both at the RAF station called Halfpenny Green (I believe that after the war this station was used in the famous film "The Way to the Stars") that was situated not far from Stourbridge in the West Midlands. A son, David, had been born in the following year after which Joyce received her discharge. Apparently her husband had not enjoyed very good health in the early years of their marriage and had required treatment at a hospital in the London area, following which they had settled in Manchester. Joyce and Bill had lived in the district of Longsight and I remember her telling me that the actor John Thaw, when a boy, had lived nearby. Seemingly he was quite a pest in that he would sit on the garden wall and had been quite cheeky! At about that time he broke a leg at school which rather curbed his activities. It's hard to believe that he is now dead after such a wonderful career.

I gathered that shortly after marriage in the 1960's, Joyce's husband had died leaving her a widow at about the age of nearly 40. Unfortunately family disagreements did not lead to a happy life at that time for Joyce and she returned to live with her mother in Handsworth Wood until our marriage in April 1979. Therefore at the ages of 56 and 59 respectively Joyce and I set out on our life together which I believe was a very happy one, and would last for almost 30 years. Obviously it was a different marriage for me than that with Helen, but in life I have learned never to compare ladies, especially when they are really close to you, to do so could cause trouble! Nowadays at the age of ninety-three, married for the third time, an Englishman living in Scotland, with liberal views on life, I have become very much a diplomat of the first order, charming to all at all times! People I have met outside Birmingham have always made fun of the Birmingham accent and of course Joyce had an accent. From time to time I would make a joke about it with her, even imitating some of her expressions which always made her laugh. But she maintained that being born in West Bromwich she was not from Birmingham but from the Black Country! Joyce and I visited my mother in Wells at regular intervals but by this time she had to give up living alone and had moved into a nursing home. She had now reached the age of over 83 and had become extremely frail, but I am sure she enjoyed our visits and loved being pushed around the streets of Wells for an hour or two in a chair. I think she enjoyed Joyce's company more than Helen's (obviously accents had a lot to do with it!) Following our very enjoyable honeymoon in July the rest of 1979 went by fairly rapidly. Apart from my day-to-day work in the Regional Office, I had on occasion to go and visit various branch offices which came under our Midland regional jurisdiction. On these occasions I sometimes had to be away for a day or two and as a recently married couple, my return was always very enjoyable! To come home to a wife for me was a necessity of life, I don't think I was ever meant to live alone; maybe my years as a prisoner of war made companionship a number one priority.

The next year came and passed by far too slowly for I was now 60 years of age and eligible for retirement which I was looking forward to avidly. One of the pastimes which I was keen to take up was as an amateur artist; years ago at the grammar school I had achieved a credit in art and it had always been in my mind that fellow POWs such as Jack Chalker and Ronald Searle seemed to get a great deal of satisfaction from their artwork. In the years to come I dabbled away producing works in watercolour, oils and acrylic, maybe they were not all that great, but friends seemed to like them so they made great gifts! Joyce and I enjoyed the house in Solihull which of course I had bought for Helen but within a year or two I fully understood that as a woman, Joyce really craved a house on which she could make her own mark. Therefore when I officially retired in October 1980 it wasn't long before we began looking for alternative accommodation, and after looking around, even as far as the Worcester area, at bungalows etc, we came to the decision to buy a modern flat, still in Solihull. Later we both agreed it was a very big mistake! Prior to moving into the flat, we enjoyed in the early summer of 1981, a holiday in London, staying for a week at a first class hotel near Charing Cross station. Joyce and I had a great time exploring the city, taking a boat trip down to Greenwich, where I happily showed her around the haunts of my childhood. We also indulged in all the usual things you do in London, afternoon tea at Fortnum and Mason, the Tower of London and of course Joyce revelled in shopping in the big stores. However the highlight turned out to be the parade for the Trooping of the Colour on the Queen's official birthday. We found a place to view, on the steps which led up to Waterloo Place, from which we could see most of The Mall leading in to Horse Guards Parade. It was a beautiful day and the Queen came by, riding her favourite horse; just as she was opposite us, a young man stepped out and fired shots at her. Naturally the horse was startled, but the Queen kept it under control and simply rode on into Horse Guards Parade, then of course all hell broke loose with a melee of police and soldiers and the young man was marched away. The episode always remained in my memory and I was interested in finding out at a later date details of "the would-be assassin". Apparently he was a Marcus Sarjeant, aged 17, seeking notoriety by firing blanks at the Queen for which he was sentenced to 5 years in jail, but was released after serving just over three years. On release apparently he changed his name after apologising for his actions and as far as I know disappeared from public life. If he's still alive he will be about 49 years of age, doing what, I should like to know.

The flat that Joyce and I moved into was brand-new, very modern and nearer Solihull town centre, it had every convenience, but it was boring and within a year or so we were looking for pastures new. Our thoughts about moving away from the Birmingham area were also coupled with the deaths of our mothers at that time. Whilst we were in Solihull we had always visited Joyce's mother once a week, either at her house or meeting her for coffee in Birmingham town centre, and of course she occasionally visited us at our house or latterly at the flat. Gwen had been a widow for a number of years, her husband had been a skilled metalworker for a large Birmingham company, and I remember Joyce had a picture of her father standing with the prop shaft which had been made for Sir Malcolm Campbell's Bluebird in which he had set the world's speed record on water. Gwen's death was in 1982 and in the next year my mother died in the nursing home in Wells, Somerset. My mother had reached the age of eighty-seven and had outlived my father by almost fifteen years, and since his death lived a rather quiet and lonely life. There is no doubt that she missed him greatly, after all, they had gone through two world wars together, had suffered the loss of siblings during the first, followed by hardship of the years before "we have never had it so good". My brother Fred came down for the funeral but we had little to talk about; I had never understood why following his divorce from his first wife Sheena MacLachlan, he had foregone all his rights to his two young children, it was something I could never have done. Therefore it follows that at my age of ninety-three, his son Malcolm English (following his mother's remarriage his surname was changed) is my only blood relative from whom I receive a yearly Christmas card. Following the death of Joyce's mother, and bearing in mind that we found the Solihull flat not to our liking, we now felt that we had more freedom in deciding where to live, and so I simply turned to Joyce and asked her for her preference. I thought it was time to dismiss Scotland from my mind and in doing so I really didn't care where I ended up. In 1983 I was in my late middle age, married to a younger woman, and quite frankly considered that I would be lucky if I made the year 2000, how wrong can you be! Joyce really only had one place in mind, namely Weston super Mare. As a schoolgirl she had been taken there by her parents on every holiday and they were the times which had given her the most happiness. I discovered that on bank holidays especially, half the population of Birmingham journeyed to "Weston", in the past by charabanc down the A4, and nowadays by car down the M5. I suppose it was popular being the nearest seaside resort, in fact for a day trip it was the only seaside resort!

Now it was a case of selling the flat and finding an abode in Weston-super-Mare and this was not going to be easy as the first and major difficulty would be in finding a buyer for the flat. I soon discovered that with regard to flats, buying is easy, selling hard work! As far as Joyce was concerned, now that she was reassured that I was happy enough to move to Weston, the move could not come quickly enough, so life became a series of weekend trips to that town. Our desired residence was a bungalow on the seafront but it soon became evident that this did not exist as the front at Western consisted of shops, hotels and amusement arcades, with bungalows at a reasonable price, only existing inland. But then one evening in the flat, reading the Birmingham evening paper, we noticed a caravan for sale at a small park in Worle, a village about three miles inland from Weston-super-Mare. Our thoughts were that this would make a base at weekends to explore the area until we were lucky enough to get a sale of the flat; once we installed ourselves in it, there was no way that Joyce was going to return to Solihull. I think that if she had been under canvas in the area she would not have moved back to Solihull, so deep was her love for Weston!

# THE SEA HAS GONE TO CARDIFF

## 1978–2008: With Joyce in Weston-super-Mare to her Death

So we moved to Weston-super-Mare, or rather just outside in Worle, where we eventually found the bungalow of Joyce's dreams, which was to be our home for almost the next 24 years. It was a happy period which unfortunately for me would again end in tears and sorrow. For me as an individual, Weston super Mare did not " hit all the buttons", it did not really face the sea but a fairly narrow stretch of the Bristol Channel, which on most days simply ebbed in and out with hardly any wave movement. However the main asset was its large wide stretches of sand which got even wider when the tide went out, eventually revealing even more stretches of mud; hence leading to the local joke. Visitor "can you tell me where the sea is? Local "it's gone to Cardiff'. The town's main asset was the pier, a magnificent construction stretching out over the sands with a large hall at the end which in the early days was the venue for shows and variety, but in recent years simply became an amusement arcade. I would imagine that in the early days it was envisaged that the end of the pier would be used as a landing stage for paddle steamers plying their trade up and down the Bristol Channel. However the shallow waters and the rise and fall of the tide meant that the time slot for calling at

Weston was limited, accordingly the addition of the extension to the pier served no purpose and in due course it was demolished. Joyce and I found our bungalow in Worle by chance. After almost a year in the caravan the flat in Solihull was sold, but finding a suitable bungalow was not easy. However one evening about 5 p.m. we took a stroll along Worle High Street and spotted 15 Annandale Avenue which was to be our home until after the turn of the century; with the name Annandale I would always be connected to Scotland! The bungalow was compact and had a moderately sized garden, not enough for vegetables but before long I had a great display of roses of all kinds. My pride and joy were my yellow hedge roses of a species called "Chinatown" and in beds I had a great display of the multi-coloured "Masquerade". Even if I was not greatly enamoured with Weston-super-Mare it was a great base for exploring Somerset, exploring even further down into Devon and Cornwall and it was not long before we took a holiday down in Newquay. It was not far to visit towns and villages such as Taunton, Bridgwater, Bath, Minehead and Porlock and we spent many a pleasant day visiting such places and returning back happy to our pretty bungalow in the evening. It was a happy life with very few commitments. Joyce, who in her early years had been a useful piano player, now purchased a small Hammond organ and became quite proficient with it, whilst I myself pursued my artistic endeavours turning out the odd watercolour or masterpiece in oils! I even tried to teach Joyce how to drive, the expanse of the beach at Weston seemed an ideal place to do this, so early one morning with the beach deserted we gave it a go. It turned out a disaster, Joyce unfortunately did not have the coordination to be a driver and although we had hundreds of yards in all directions in which to manoeuvre, at one point we found ourselves heading for the sea at what seemed to me a hundred miles per hour. Our nerves were shattered but were restored by parking the car (by me!) and enjoying coffee and a bun in a restaurant. Learning to drive was a subject never raised again! I have passed comment previously that Joyce had left her family commitments in Manchester following disagreement with her son and his wife. It was a topic which I felt I should steer clear of as it was one of which I had no direct knowledge. Apparently however, not long after our marriage, her son David tried to make contact by corresponding via Barry, Joyce's brother. Knowing the situation between Joyce and her family, Barry asked me to try and resolve the situation, which I did by writing to David advising him of his mother's remarriage and putting myself forward as an avenue for any future communication. As time went by the rift did ease a little and in the years to come her family came down to see her on one or two occasions, the visits passing off reasonably well, although most of the time they were a few and far between.

I was now approaching my 70s, luckily still enjoying relatively good health and hopeful that with any luck I might see the year 2000; Joyce and I were living a blissful existence, no worries from either our health or a monetary point of view, which I suppose was why we both tended to put on a little extra weight. We occasionally went back to visit our old stomping grounds in Birmingham and in West Bromwich, where she had attended the grammar school in her youth, and later on was employed by Webley and Scott. She was of course a supporter of West Bromwich Albion during those years and she recalled that a great friend of hers had been a landlady for a young up and coming footballer called Bobby Robson, who in later years became one of England's greatest football managers. My only connection with Scotland at this time came with the occasional visit by my nephew Kenneth Reid who as a financial consultant had business from time to time in the Bristol area and needless to say I was extremely pleased to see him. However my peaceful world was soon to be shattered with the news of my brother's death in Cockermouth, at the age of sixty-five. Apparently he had retired at that age from his job in the Post Office and had suffered a heart attack within a few weeks; this news was difficult to comprehend as apparently at that time he was extremely fit, leading an outdoor life. I had little contact with my brother since my mother's death but of course I travelled up for his funeral in Cockermouth and it was heartening to be made aware of the esteem that Fred's colleagues had for him; at the same time I got to know more about Fred's second wife Hazel who surprisingly, turned out to be quite different from what I expected. She was a mild and softly spoken person with a gentle manner and after returning to Weston I corresponded with her from time to time, and in fact in later years when she died I felt obliged to return to Cockermouth for her funeral. I've always felt a little sad about my brother, I don't think he was ever satisfied with his life achievements, but perhaps from his and Hazel's point of view they had a happy marriage even though both of them had in a way walked away from commitments to the children of their first marriages.

Again I return to my idyllic life in Annandale Avenue; however my comfort was soon to be shattered. One morning I woke up and found I could not move without getting an excruciating pain in my back; Joyce summoned our doctor who ordered an ambulance for me to be carted away to the local hospital. I arrived at the hospital at about 10a.m. and spent the next seven hours on a trolley in a corridor, where I was given an injection and provided I didn't move a muscle the pain was not quite so severe. I understood at the time that efforts were made to find a bed for me, but to no avail, and so in the early evening a doctor diagnosed that I probably had a slipped disc, gave me a hefty dose of painkiller and sent me back home by ambulance. I was treated at home with more strong painkillers and after about a week I was able to move reasonably freely. I attended the hospital as an outpatient for quite a time under the care of a senior physiotherapist, who eventually arranged my attendance at a "Back School" run by a very proficient lady called Miss Hatton, who in my opinion would have made a very suitable member of the wartime Gestapo. At my first session at the "school" I was stretched on a wooden frame with my shoulders and ankles firmly fastened, following which the top and bottom halves of the frame were slowly pulled apart, apparently the idea being that the pressure on my spine would be relieved. Further lessons mainly consisted of lying on the wooden floor and stretching various parts of the body in all sorts of directions. Needless to say I was very grateful when after three weeks I was discharged from being one of Miss Hatton's patients. However by now I was able to move reasonably freely but the hospital issued me with a straitjacket (technically a medical corset) which I was advised should be worn whenever I undertook any strenuous work, this gave me a marvellous excuse in future years for avoiding jobs which did not appeal to me. To this day I still get a twinge of sciatica from time to time from which I get relief by using a homoeopathic remedy called "Devils claw".

By now you have probably guessed that I am not particularly enthusiastic about attending hospitals and if possible I refrain from visiting doctors. Possibly my experiences as a prisoner of war is the reason for this (if you reported sick and went to the hospital hut you were put on half rations and probably died there); at ninety-three years of age I have no major health problems and take no prescribed medication for which I am extremely grateful. I would like to reach the age of a hundred so that despite the efforts of the Japanese military, I would reach a pinnacle in life that is respected by all, and certainly in Japan itself. The pleasant years in Somerset went by, there is no doubt that for Joyce those years up to the time she reached age eighty were the most enjoyable of her life. She was living a worry free time in a place she loved, all she wanted was there for her in Weston-super-Mare, and in a way I too was happy in knowing that. Maybe looking back now, the years from my age of eighty were for me a little dull in that I was living too much a comfortable life with a lack of purpose, which may sound peculiar to a lot of people who reached the age of eighty, but then and even now 13 years later I feel that life can be dull if you let it. By the end of the century Joyce had lost her enthusiasm for her music; she had started off just after we were married by purchasing a small Hammond organ, and after mastering it she obtained a replacement in the form of a larger state of the art Japanese instrument. This in turn made way for an upright piano which in a way suited her, bearing in mind the certificates she had obtained in her youth for proficiency in pianoforte. In due course, all the musical instruments were sold, Joyce being content in the evening to watch the television. To my way of thinking this was a great pity as I am a great believer that in order to keep mind and body active a hobby or activity is a great asset. I myself had the garden to keep me busy; I took an active interest in the fortunes of Weston-super-Mare football club and of course I still practiced my artistic skills, turning out from time to time paintings in oil and acrylic. A good number of my artistic efforts were given away to friends but many were hung on the walls of the bungalow, to my mind they were not worth selling, however friends did seem to appreciate them.

In due course life in Weston-super-Mare reached the millennium. Looking back I cannot remember that we greeted the dawn of 2001 with any great enthusiasm, which for me was quite remarkable bearing in mind that in my youth and middle age I had very grave doubts that I would ever reach it, but I did and I was 80 and reasonably fit, good on you Jack! In January 2001 I was surprised to receive a communication from the government (war pensions agency) to the effect that Ex-Far East prisoners of war were to receive an ex-gratia payment of £10,000, subject to my making a satisfactory claim, and in due course that amount made its way into my bank account. I can only assume that the government had acquired after all the passing years, a guilty conscience. Thinking back I seem to remember that sometime after the war the Emperor of Japan had paid a visit to London as a guest of the Queen, a visit that did not meet with universal approval (maybe Earl Mountbatten and the Duke of Edinburgh were not all that happy) so perhaps this had some bearing. The war against Japan had ceased nearly 56 years ago, many of the survivors had since died, I personally was over 80 and in anybody's book the payment, whatever the amount, should have been paid by the Japanese government as quickly as possible after the end of the war, together with an appropriate apology for the suffering of the prisoners. The payment was £10,000, quite a reasonable sum and no one was going to look a gift horse in the mouth but had even £500 being paid in 1946 to the survivors they would have helped in a far greater way. I don't know what my fellow survivors did with the money; I suppose it would depend on the circumstances they were in. I would like to think that like myself, they were comfortably situated in which case they probably treated themselves to a fine holiday; my £10,000 stayed in the bank for a rainy day and 11 years later it's still there!

In April 2004 Joyce and I celebrated our silver wedding anniversary with a few close friends and family in our bungalow in Annandale Avenue. It was a quiet affair as Joyce who had now reached the age of eighty-one, was beginning to show signs of deteriorating health. She had been diagnosed with angina and heart trouble and from time to time needed the help of a visiting nurse. However we enjoyed the day and as we looked back over the past twenty-five years we both felt the time had been one of peace and happiness and so had passed by quite rapidly. My own thoughts dwelt in realising that I had been a participant in two silver weddings and was now 84, to quote a popular phrase "I don't believe it"! Soon Joyce was beginning to suffer a lack of mobility and in order for her to enjoy her daily visits into Weston-super-Mare I purchased a folding wheelchair which I could take in the car into the town thus enabling her to be wheeled along the promenade. Weston-super-Mare was a town with a fairly large proportion of retired people, and a good number of them required mobility aids of various kinds. I must say that the local council facilities were first class, lowered kerbs on pavements, slopes as alternatives to steps and disabled toilet facilities were excellent. The next couple of years were difficult but we managed reasonably well, and we were lucky in that we had a bungalow with every facility on the ground floor and things were made easier by installing a "wet room" in the bathroom. However with the angina and poor blood circulation Joyce began to suffer from ulcerated legs which along with lack of movement required nurses to visit on a regular basis.

Eventually about 2006/7 Joyce was admitted to the local hospital and unfortunately was not able to return to the bungalow again. Hospitals at that time had their difficulties, they were lacking in sufficient numbers of trained staff and even the auxiliary nurses, who in the main were from abroad, were in short supply. The wards contained both male and female patients which led to a lack of privacy which did not go down well at all. However after a month of two this was resolved and by the middle of 2007 Joyce had been moved into a private room. Luckily there were few restrictions on visiting so I was able to turn up prior to the main meal times and help to feed Joyce, as when time went by, she found it difficult to manage utensils. I was pleased to be able to do this as from time to time I noticed that food had been left in front of other patients, and later they had been removed uneaten. I was lucky that I still had my car and able to drive to and back from the hospital about three times a day but I must admit that at the end of each day I was feeling my years. Despite hospital care and attention Joyce's condition did not improve, in fact it was deteriorating in that she was confined to her bed and had to be lifted from it by special apparatus when the bedding had to be changed. She was now suffering from acute arteriosclerosis which was affecting most of her body and naturally I was extremely worried regarding lack of improvement in her condition. To this end I sought interviews with doctors and consultants in the hope that they could offer some assurance that there would be some improvement in the future. Most times this proved difficult as enquiries never got further than the ward sister, who could only elaborate on Joyce's current condition, the doctor not being available, probably due to pressure of work. This situation continued for quite a long time until I finally did get a meeting with a senior doctor who more or less told me that there was little chance of Joyce making any improvement not long after this meeting I was informed that as the hospital could not do any more for Joyce they felt that her well-being would be best served by her moving into a nursing home. Of course I was not happy about this and I had further meetings with social services to discuss the possibility of Joyce receiving nursing at home. However they would not contemplate this course of action, pointing out that as I was now over the age of eighty-seven I would be incapable of attending to Joyce, also the cost of 24-hour nursing had to be ruled out.

I was given a list of suitable nursing homes and more or less given a deadline by which time Joyce had to be moved. In due course I did find a suitable home, one which was not far from the bungalow and where Joyce would have her own room equipped with the necessary lifting apparatus. In view of the attention that Joyce needed I was surprised that, on assessment she was deemed not severe enough a case to have the nursing home fees paid for by the NHS, and accordingly the full cost would have to be borne by myself. I was concerned that Joyce would receive the best attention possible, the nursing home was excellent, so I accepted the monetary burden without quibble. It is interesting to see that five years later the NHS in similar cases were being challenged using legal aid, but in 2007

I suppose we just accepted what we were told. And so in that year Joyce moved into the nursing home, which was situated on the slopes of Worlebury Hill looking down on the town and I would like to think that for the most part she was happy there. For me there was little change in my routine, I went to the home at the main meal times to help her and keep her company just as I did at the hospital; I had a good rapport with the staff who also gave me my meals which I suppose made life easier for me. Family visitors to Joyce in hospital had been few and far between and this was also the position regarding the nursing home, in a way this was understandable as we were quite a distance away from them in Weston. Joyce's brother Barry managed to get to see her on a number of occasions but her son David, as far as I can remember, averaged about one visit per year. The rest of 2007 passed by, not a very happy time. Looking back I hope I did my best for Joyce but for the both of us it was a lonely time. I don't think that time was an issue with Joyce as her condition was such that she spent a great deal of time sleeping and showed little interest in watching the television in her room. I personally used to leave the nursing home about 7 p.m. when the staff began settling the patients for the night and when I reached the bungalow I really did spend some miserable evenings. Christmas came and went, I cannot remember much about it, I suppose there were decorations at the Nursing Home and everyone did their best to be cheerful but it really was not the time for merriment. Little did I know what 2008 would bring and it was just as well. After Christmas it was the week which ran up to Hogmanay, the last day of 2007 I shall never forget. I went to the nursing home about my usual time of 11a.m. but had to wait in the residents lounge for a while as the nurses were attending to

Joyce. Eventually I got to her room and sat beside her for a chat before lunch was being brought in, she was very quiet and only spoke a few words and ate very little of the meal when it was put before her. After a few more words she dropped off to sleep so I just sat beside her reading a newspaper for an hour or so in case she woke up again for a talk. Joyce was still sleeping when I left just after 3 p.m. and when I returned at 5 p.m. for the evening meal she again was not very talkative and again was not inclined to take hardly any nourishment. The nurses came up to the room between 6 p.m. and 7 p.m. to make her comfortable for the night and as she had fallen asleep again I left to go back to the bungalow. I woke up on New Year's Day 2008 at my usual time of 7 a.m. and after a quick shower was sitting down for breakfast when the phone rang. It was the matron at the nursing home to give me the news that Joyce had died in the early hours of the morning.

I went up to the nursing home to find staff there sympathetic and had already completed the necessary arrangements. Joyce looked at peace and although I had lost her, I felt her suffering was at an end. I could not understand why fate should decree that at the age of almost 88, for the second time, I should lose a companion in life who had meant so much to me. With Council Offices closed it was not possible to register the death until 3 January, or of course make funeral arrangements, but there were all the necessary phone calls to be made to friends and relatives; being by myself, this I found extremely distressing. Some years previously when drawing up our wills we had provisionally discussed burial when such a time came, but a few months prior to her death whilst in hospital she told me that if she predeceased me she wished to be cremated; apparently she was fearful of being buried alive, all my assurances to her on this point failed and so her wishes were carried out. The funeral service was carried out about a week later with the coffin being kept open until about three hours before the service in case her family wished to see her for the final time, but to my knowledge this was not taken advantage of. A few days after the service at the crematorium I was able to make the lonely journey to collect Joyce's ashes and scatter them in the garden of remembrance. This is what I'm sure she would have wanted; she loved Weston-super-Mare from when she was a child until the day she passed away. She did not love the Manchester area and in due course fell out of love with Birmingham. I too now had a lot to think about, as I said before, Weston-super-Mare in my language was not "my cup of tea" and I had no love for big cities, what now would be before me? My nephew Kenneth Reid had come down for the funeral and I had been very pleased to see him as of course he had been my link with Scotland and his aunt Helen all those years ago. I believe that he was interested in what I was going to do with my life but of course it was early days and I needed time to get over the loss of Joyce.

The spring of the year went by and on 15 April I reached age eighty-eight, to me it was a case of "the wonders will never cease". Surely at my age another move was out of the question, everyone tells you that moving house is the most worrying time in anyone's life, and as far as worries are concerned I felt I had already had my fair share of those. However, in May an advert in the local paper indicated that a company called McCarthy and Stone were building a complex of flats in the Worle area and I was interested enough to learn what was on offer. It seemed that life in a self-contained flat on a managed basis seemed to offer a worry free existence for the rest of any life I could expect. Then I thought, why not find out if the same facility exists in Scotland? Maybe in Peebles? Further enquiries revealed that McCarthy and Stone did have plans in that area and that every help would be given to me in moving north. I decided to make the plunge and put the bungalow on the market, a move which unfortunately coincided with the recession and a fall in house values. In the end faced with only one offer, I reluctantly accepted it, even though it was below the figure I wished for, but by hook or by crook I was now determined to get back to Scotland. I now had to vacate the bungalow by midsummer but my plans went a bit astray when I discovered that the complex in Peebles had hardly been started and that entry into it was not likely to be available until early 2009. I did not relish putting my furniture and belongings into storage for about nine months so I had a chat on the phone with my nephew Kenneth and he gave me a solution, why not move to Largs? Apparently Kenneth had discovered that McCarthy and Stone had just completed a complex of flats at the North Ayrshire seaside town and as it was a town about the size of Peebles, he thought that it might appeal to me. Whilst I was contemplating this suggestion, the purchaser of my bungalow was anxious to get possession as soon as possible. Apparently he had bought it for the use of his disabled son and was anxious to put plans before the local authority for certain alterations to be made, to enable the lad, who was confined to a wheelchair, to spend a normal a life as possible. After great deliberation I thought why not Largs? After all it was Scotland, and visiting Peebles from time to time would not be difficult, therefore I phoned the appropriate number in Largs to ascertain what was on the market. I required a two bedroomed flat and was informed that two flats were left, one on the first floor and a ground floor one which was not yet available as it was being used as a show flat, but it was possible it would be released soon. I was invited to inspect both but to do so would have meant a round journey of between eight hundred and nine hundred miles and so I asked Kenneth and his wife Elsa to go and see them on my behalf; they lived in Glasgow and could do the trip in under an hour. In due course Kenneth plumped for the first floor flat which had a balcony but Elsa made a point that with Scottish weather the open balcony with luck, might only be usable for three months in the year; in addition she pointed out that the show flat was fully completed, fitted with fireplace, lighting, mirrors and curtains etc and was ready for immediate entry when released. On the premise that women in these matters are more knowledgeable and additionally the flat with a balcony was £40,000 more I went with Elsa's choice, a decision I did not regret. The chosen flat was released to me and with trepidation I arranged my move back to Scotland. I knew that in modern parlance I had to downsize which I managed to do with the help of a plan of the flat; it's amazing what you collect over the years, so of course the local charity shop benefited. Along with the odd bits of furniture that went, about a dozen pictures, painted by me in various mediums, were also gifted to charity and I trust they did benefit from their sale, I hoped some people appreciated them! I did take one oil of a Clipper in full sail to the Atlantic fish restaurant in Weston-super-Mare as a present for the delightful meals Joyce and I had there in past years; a friend who went to the restaurant just last year reported that the picture was still holding a pride of place! At midday on a Monday in July following the departure of the furniture van, I drove up Worle High Street, handed the bungalow keys to the estate agent and headed northwards on the M5. I had left Scotland in 1973 and now 35 years later I was going back to take up permanent residence there. It would not be the same as 1947, how could it be? 61 years ago Helen was waiting for me, but at least I was back to where for me life was more pleasurable, even at the age of eighty-eight. Whatever life now had in store for me I would make the best of it, maybe the future would hold some surprises, I was always the optimist!

# LIVING IN LARGS

During that Monday I made my way up the M5, joined the M6 and managed to reach Lancaster in the evening for bed and breakfast. Off again on Tuesday morning, over the Scottish border at Carlisle, on through Kilmarnock finally coming down onto the North Ayrshire coast and arriving in Largs about 2 p.m. It was a beautiful sunny day, the town looked marvellous and with the calm sea and blue sky I could not have asked for a better welcome. I parked the car on the front, ambled into the local hostelry (The George), had a great lunch and then made my way up to the block of flats which was to be my home in the future. I was received at Cumbrai Court by Rosie, who up to then had only been known to me on the telephone, and as my belongings would not arrive until the next morning she very kindly put me up in one of the unsold flats, which was now acting as the show flat. The next morning the removal men arrived and in less than two hours everything was in and I was fully installed in flat number 3. Of course it took me several days to sort my belongings out into their final resting places and if I may say so this was accomplished by this old man in a tidy and methodical manner; from an old army sergeant you would not expect less. There followed the exploration of my surroundings, starting with Cumbrae Court itself, paying particular attention to the layout of its facilities. Looking around the town of Largs itself would occupy my time over the following weeks, with my attention focused on getting to know some of the townsfolk, in addition of course to fellow residents of Cumbrae Court. In 1940 after unpacking a 15 hundredweight wireless truck, I had gone across the street in Peebles to buy my newspaper and had met Helen. In 2008 after unpacking I did the same thing, meeting in the corner shop, a very charming lady called Kirsty, but on this occasion the consequences were not the same, I was just a tad too old, although over the years that followed we became great friends.

Of course I made it my priority to get acquainted with other existing flat holders, and over the following months I got to know Cathy, Sheena, Win, Betty, Auld Jock, Olive, Jessie and Angus, amongst many other good friends. The flats were for retired people who had reached at least the age of fifty-five and though very much capable of looking after themselves wanted freedom from the chores of maintaining property. The complex was not a large one, it had been scaled down due to ground area being lost to the redevelopment of the very famous Italian ice cream parlour and restaurant called Nardini's. This development was supported by the local council, the original Nardini's had been well known all over Scotland, and in particular in the Glasgow area which only being one hour's distance by coach or car, was the source of day trippers to Largs, thus bringing welcome cash. The flats had a daytime manager, Jim, who over time I got to know very well. In his spare time he was an enthusiastic bowler (not as in cricket but the other type aimed at a jack), cricket is not really recognised in Scotland, it's their loss! Jim and I eventually formed a partnership, investing once a week in what is known up here as "the fixed odds", which was betting on results of football matches, football (Association) being the principal sporting activity in the area. The return on our investments was poor at first but improved when tactics were altered. We found that English matches were better judged by Jim (a Scot) whilst I as a Sassenach I excelled with the Scottish, the less you know the better! Further north you might come across other peculiar games, Shinty and Curling, but as far as I know these do not involve wagering! Oh I almost forgot there is golf, in which I became very proficient before I retired, but I think betting in golf matches only came about on a man to man basis, in my case this involved buying a round of drinks. Ken and Elsa came down on the following weekend to see that I had settled in all right and I took them for a meal at Morris's restaurant just a few yards away along the main road. I had discovered the restaurant within a day or two and had made friends with the proprietor Gordon, who had created a decor in the establishment based on types of the old Morris minor cars, hence the name of the restaurant. I also frequented a small bistro called the Gypsy Cream, run by James, who dished up some great food, including magnificent soups made by his charming petite wife and here I had many morning coffees and lunches. After a time some of the residents at Cumbrae Court got together on a Thursday afternoon for afternoon tea and chat, and I must say that the topics discussed covered an enormous range of subjects, some of which even for me, were quite bizarre and sometimes a little "near the knuckle". Not long after I had settled in, the complex was officially opened on 8 August 2008 by the Scottish actress Dorothy Paul, the ceremony taking place at an afternoon tea party. As a Londoner I must admit that her name did not ring a bell but when we were gathered in the lounge I was aware of a very vivacious lady standing beside me and I wondered who the new resident could be. Later on the same lady turned out to be Dorothy and it was charming of her to remark that she had appreciated standing beside a tall, handsome, gentleman. I felt it only right to reply that she herself scrubbed up well! At a later date my friend Gordon of Morris's restaurant obtained for me one of Dorothy's DVDs which enabled me to appreciate her artistry. We were a group of retired people who between us had great knowledge of life, we were far from our dotage and we had opinions on every subject under the sun. On many occasions the residents lounge rocked with laughter as everyone put in their pennyworth to the conversation. Auld Jock was noted for his off the cuff remarks, and I remember when he got a new hearing aid (he was apt on occasion to misunderstand what had been said and his reply would cause great hilarity), he praised the model he had received from the NHS as being far superior to a private one costing hundreds of pounds. Apparently with the NHS apparatus he could hear his fish swimming in their tank, so on occasion he had to take out the new aid to give his ears a rest! Of course flats at Cumbrae Court had only been available from towards the end of 2007 and although the two-bedroomed ones had gone quite quickly, the sale of single bedrooms went slowly. I could never understand why companies who built these complexes never increased the percentage of available two bedroomed flats; people who retire from their houses still need some space. I arrived in 2008 preceded by, I think, about five or six residents and after that and up to the present day people still arrived; quoting Eric Morecambe's "as follows but not necessarily in the right order" they were, Mary and Peter, Norman and Jean, Jenny, Bob, Jean Inglis, Maybeth, May Bell, Bill, Hugh, Margaret and also

Evelyn. There are other residents and we will come across them at a later date but at this time mention must be given to Margaret Aitken who retired from a senior position in the nursing service. With her expertise she was able to deal with McCarthy and Stone and the managing agents Peverel and on behalf of the residents, you might say she was an excellent unpaid secretary. Evelyn Hood came, as many did from the Paisley area and was a well-known author with numerous books depicting life in times gone by in that area. In writing this book Evelyn has been helpful to me on more than one occasion and since she has promised not to sue on its publication I am happy to confirm (I'm a coward) that she is both beautiful and talented! Early on in my life at Cumbrae Court Jim asked me that in the event of a fire alarm at the complex sounding off would I reset the alarm system after the Fire Brigade had been? I agreed which leads me to Sheena who I had met on her arrival to take up residence. Sheena had been resident in Switzerland and had worked originally for the United Nations, and I happened to be at the front door when she arrived. Being helpful, I showed her the way to her flat, put her in the picture as to the layout of the complex, adding that if she needed help, Jack was available. That evening she knocked on the door of number four, answered by Cathie, who was asked to convey her thanks to her husband. Cathie told her in no uncertain terms I was not, and not likely to be, ever! I think Sheena from that first day onwards regarded me with more than a little suspicion. However back to the fire alarm; sometime later, one evening we were all aware that there was a great deal of smoke drifting round the corridors and in addition lights were flickering, accordingly the alarm was sounded. Apparently we should have all stayed in our flats, (each was fitted with a fireproof door) but everyone congregated in the lounge to welcome the firemen, whereupon I assumed that in my status given to me by Jim, I should take a roll call. In my authoritative London accent I called out the Scottish names to discover all present except for Sheena! We were on the point of organising a search party when a figure appeared outside the front door in the car park. It was Sheena complete with what appeared to be half of her belongings. When we let her in she answered our enquiries by telling us that she had made her way down the stairs from the top floor, out the back emergency door to the car park, and in her opinion that's where we all should have been! My composure was not improved by Cathie remarking on the shape of my legs (I had a short dressing gown over shorty pyjamas).

House owners are probably aware that newly built properties are never a hundred percent perfect, there are always defects, possibly minor, that require putting right within a guarantee period. Complexes are of the same nature and Cumbrae Court was no exception in that over the next two or three years several aspects of the building proved to be defective, all of which in time were put right. However later in the winter, one major defect was brought to light after a period of stormy weather, which resulted in the complex being reroofed following discussion between McCarthy and Stone and a contractor (the effort of Margaret Aitken in this matter was noteworthy). It was natural for the residents who were already in situ to voice their concerns regarding the building and at our weekly tea party these worries tended to be joked about giving rise to the renaming between ourselves of our abode, which we all now called "Crumbly Court"! We were lucky to have Betty as a resident, she came with two pianos!

One was placed in the residents lounge and was handy for the occasional singsong. In my opinion Betty had the best flat in the building, apparently it was formed from a part of the new building and a bit left over from a previous one; accordingly it was the largest and had views in several directions. I gathered from Betty that the flat was offered to her as an afterthought following her initial enquiry, if so she hit the jackpot, it accommodated all her belongings plus the other piano! Christmas 2008 arrived and of course most residents were away to relatives, and I myself joined Ken and Elsa with their sons at their home in Bearsden (Glasgow) for a very pleasant and relaxing time. Most people were back before the New Year so many of us congregated in the lounge for a party on Hogmanay. Betty belatedly thumped out the old Christmas tunes and when we got to Jingle Bells I was happy to accompany her with my two hand bells, which for some reason I had brought with me from England! Normal bedtime for many was about 10 p.m. and as the party had started before 6 p.m. it was decided that festivities would be adjourned at nine o'clock but everyone would come back just before midnight to see the New Year in. Accordingly at 11.45 p.m. I paraded along the corridors of all the floors, ringing my bells to summon all to fall in for the toast! The winter of 2008/9 was pretty tempestuous, I gathered that Largs was well-known for the strength of the westerly gales and the residents in the top floor felt, at times, that the roof was on its way to America, and in fact the noise and vibration resulted in the roof being replaced as mentioned earlier.

Commencing in early 2009 there were from time to time obituaries appearing in the Daily Telegraph relating to ex-Japanese prisoners of war and since I did not take the newspaper, fellow residents Angus and Jessie kindly drew my attention to them. I am sure they were not trying to cheer me up! The service men had died before reaching ninety years of age and this set me thinking, I would be eighty-nine in April and for years I had harboured the notion to return to Thailand and see the railway again. Now I was in a position to do so, being once again a widower, able to afford the journey and make it before I reached the age of ninety. I talked about it with my friends in the Court who encouraged me to take steps to bring it about, my next-door neighbour Cathie pointing out that if I did not do the trip I might regret it for the rest of life that was left. I hotfooted it down to "Largs Travel", sat in front of a lassie called Vannah and said, "I want to go to Singapore, then take the Eastern Oriental Express to Bangkok calling at Kanchanaburi (Bridge on the River Kwai) before finally coming home." I suppose it was a little out of the ordinary from a week on the Costa Del Sol, especially coming from a 90-year-old pensioner, leaning on his stick, and prepared to travel alone, but Vannah didn't turn a hair. In a matter of a few days it was all arranged, first-class travel and I would be cared for on every stage of the journey, which would take place, providing I'm still alive, next October. Needless to say my proposed trip was a subject for debate at our Thursday afternoon tea parties, advice was plentiful, many were seasoned travellers, may be only as far as Europe, but all felt I needed guidance! My friends already knew of my experiences during the war from past conversations and felt, as I probably did, that conditions in the Far East had not changed very much; accordingly advice was given as to the best methods to be adopted to keep one's smalls in good condition, plus hints on hygiene! Well before my departure date Win (one of the original "inmates"), supplied me with a substantial case with wheels and for quite a considerable time reminded me at every opportunity about the inoculations I should be taking. At this time I was reminded by the DVLA that my driving licence was due for renewal and as I had rarely used the car since arriving in Largs I decided it was time to stop driving. Kenneth had experienced trouble with his own car so I was happy to pass mine on to him, it wasn't exactly new but it's mileage was reasonably low. Ken and Elsa came down during the summer at regular intervals and were kind enough to take me on several trips, which included Cumbrae and Millport, also Arran, a visit which I found to be delightful.

I think it was about the end of July or possibly the beginning of August when I met for the first time Mrs Mary Mees. On this particular Thursday I needed some provisions before having a spot of lunch at the "Gypsy Cream", this of course prior to the afternoon tea party at the Court. Mary and I met by accident at the supermarket checkout. I had picked up a chocolate bar at the counter, but on second thoughts replaced it, to be complimented by Mary on my willpower, following which we had a little chat on the pavement outside. During our conversation I remarked that I had moved in to a McCarthy and Stone development, flat number 3 to be precise, to which Mary warily stated that her flat was similarly addressed, how come? It turned out that Mary was not aware of the new development and I of the old McCarthy and Stone complex built 25 years ago on the other side of the town. Once all suspicions were erased I thought it was a good time to suggest that we could continue our chat the following week, of course on Thursday, over a bowl of soup, at the "Gypsy Cream", still leaving me free on that day for the afternoon tea party! Most people quite rightly would consider that kind of invitation a pretty poor effort, quite rightly so, and when the time came I expected to lunch by myself and later I learned that Mary was inclined at first to give it a miss. I was lucky when she did turn up. This was the beginning of our friendship, and we met on a regular basis enjoying each other's company and I discovered that she had been a widow for a number of years and had moved to Largs just a short time previous. The trip to Thailand was still very much on my mind but Mary and I still found time to enjoy each other's company, having meals together, talking about our past lives, which surprisingly appeared at times to have been spent in identical areas. Mary and her late husband had lived in Long Ashton (a village between Weston-super-Mare and Bristol) when I too was in that area, later on as a widow she had moved back to Scotland, and even for a time contemplated living in Peebles! Later on in August I was introduced by Mary to her friend of many years, namely Janet Lampert and it was from her and other friends that I learned that everyone else referred to Mary as Maddie, in fact I had been far too formal! From the time of initially meeting Maddie, to setting forth on my trip, we were only together for perhaps a matter of two months, but there is no doubt our friendship blossomed during that time. We had a great deal in common, humour, outlook on life and common interests and as far as I was concerned life was dull between meetings, each time I could hardly wait to see her again. I discovered that Maddie had been born Mary Margaret MacGilp and lived in her youth in Tighnabruaich (please don't ask me to pronounce it!), a village situated in the Iyles of Bute, Argyllshire. Proving to my Scottish friends that I have a knowledge of Rabbie Burns, to me Maddie was my "Mary of Argyll", and very bonny to! By the time my departure to the Far East had come, my love for Maddie had become quite deep and sincere and I left on my journey very hopeful that on my return the friendship would develop further, I was smitten!

# BACK TO THE KWAI

## 2009: After 64 years I return

Time was now approaching for my journey to the Far East, with knowledge of it reaching the local newspaper and the publicity department of McCarthy and Stone. This gave rise to a half page article in the local weekly newspaper with the captions "Jack the Lad" and "Largs POW returning to the River Kwai", together with an article in the Scottish field magazine headed "never too old". Both articles emphasised my age but thankfully made it clear that I was far from decrepit with no hint of senility! Therefore in October I set off to go back in time, 64 years almost to the day, and I was ready, all inoculations done, all necessary required currency (Dubai dollars, Singapore dollars, Thai bahts, American dollars and of course Sterling.) The Airline (Emirates) were not going to convey me without insurance, especially an old bugger nearly 90, who could easily expire somewhere on the River Kwai. The insurance was a little costly, however needs must! So with Win's case packed to bursting and dressed ready for the tropics, (clothing by the Tilley Company of Canada) I turned up at Glasgow airport on Saturday, 3rd October 2009 to catch the 14.15 plane for Dubai. I should also say that a few of the residents at the Court were kind enough to see me off on my way, maybe they thought there was a hopeful possibility that I would not make it back! Previous air travel by myself had been confined to trips between Birmingham and Edinburgh, therefore long distant journeys were a new experience for me. The interior of the plane seemed vast but the seats were extremely comfortable and the in-flight entertainment excellent, although I was more intrigued with the screen in front of me plotting the position of the plane on its journey! After excellent meals served by stewardesses in a kind of oriental uniform I was able to doze for an hour or two before landing, just after midnight at Dubai. After about two hours in a holding lounge it was on to a plane for Singapore, again with efficiency by the airline, although I did worry about my luggage which I had not seen since leaving Glasgow, no need to panic!

We touched down at Singapore's Changi airport in the early afternoon which gave me cause for reflection. The last time I had been on this stretch of ground it had been a Japanese military airfield and I, along with other poor wretches were labouring levelling the runway. No longer was I seeing a line of zero fighters along the airfield boundary, with the shouts of the Japanese engineers exhorting us to work harder, together with the occasional whack round the back with a bamboo stick. Now I was standing in a beautiful designed airport, a vast complex of steel, chromium, glass and tiling, it was hard to believe. I was brought to life by a petite Chinese lady bearing a placard with a message "Mr Robert Ransom – Mandarin Oriental Hotel" and of course my limousine awaited me, there was no trudge back to Changi jail! The car journey from the airport to the city centre I knew would cover a distance of about fifteen miles but I was not prepared for the change in scenery! As the car sped along a brand new motorway I was astonished by the changes in the countryside, let me correct that, there was no countryside! Where were the bits of jungle? Where were the rubber plantations? What has happened to the Kampongs at Katong and Kalang and what has happened to the Aerodrome at Kalang? It was all bewildering to me as I journeyed through roads I did not recognise in the final stage of my journey up to the hotel. The Mandarin Oriental Hotel was situated in Raffles Avenue, Marina Square, a modern building of I would think 20 floors . The hotel was sumptuous, out trotted the doorkeeper resplendent in uniform, together with two bellboys for the luggage and I was escorted into an arrival lounge as big as a football pitch, this was to be my home for the next four days.

At the reception desk I was received by the resident manager Jill Goh, who having been advised to expect a 90 year old man, struck me as being a little surprised to discover I could stand on my own two feet and move about at a reasonable speed. In fact during my stay at the Mandarin Oriental, both in Singapore and Bangkok, it seemed to be that my age and mobility was a source of wonderment to the staff, especially to the girls, who felt they had to look after me, and I am afraid I did take advantage! Everyone seemed to know the reason for my visit, news travels fast in the East! Apparently not many old soldiers from 1945 get back to Singapore in 2009, maybe I was the only one most had ever seen; one or two of the Chinese girls pointed out that it was their great grandfathers who were knocking around during the Japanese occupation; remarks of that nature made me feel really ancient! My room (complete with butler) was on the 19th floor, beautifully furnished, about the size of a tennis court, with a bed to accommodate five people, with a view to the right over Marina Bay, which years ago was the old harbour full of Chinese junks and edged with small shops and eating houses. Marina Bay was now surrounded by skyscrapers, to the south and east there were acres of land reclaimed from the sea, the Bay was cut off from the sea by an expressway bypassing the city centre and running between the East and West coasts. Also in front of my window about a quarter of a mile away was a relative of the London Eye, splendidly lit up at night, truly Singapore had changed, I could hardly believe it! Situated on the same floor as my room was the hotel's Oriental Club and as I had automatically been made a member I found it extremely useful for meals and drinks without using the main facilities. Also by using it, the hostesses there got to know me and of course look after me, in particular one charming girl called Cornelia, what more could an old chap ask for! By the time I had taken my evening meal and a nightcap in the bar, I was ready for bed, travel and the time zones had caught up with me. In any case I wanted to be fit and lively for the next three days before boarding the Eastern and Oriental express on the 8 October bound for Thailand. The next day was spent getting my bearings, Singapore for me had changed beyond recognition, all the old roads seemed to have vanished, I couldn't find the old Bukit Timah Road and when I made enquiries from passers-by I didn't get much help. Studying a map later I saw it had been replaced by a new expressway and presumably the old village had disappeared under concrete blocks of flats. I discovered that the main shopping area was along Orchard Road and eventually finding a post office in one of the malls I sent off my "wish you were here" postcards, addressing one to Win as "Dear Mum". Later that day I got a visit from Carolyn Quek, a journalist with the Straits Times, interested in why a very old man from the colonial past was back and what did he now think of Singapore? All I could say was "it's definitely changed".

Carolyn very kindly walked with me and showed me where the City Hall was situated, with the old Padang in front of it; in the old days it had been used by the cricket club, and I was surprised that it was still used for that purpose although it seemed to me that back in the 1940s, it was nearer to the harbour, maybe more reclamation had been done. Carolyn, on our walk, also pointed out the Esplanade theatres with the bridge leading to Raffles Quay and by that time I was beginning to get my bearings, at any rate with regard to the harbour area. Finally we had a cup of tea together before Carolyn had to return to her office and during that time she asked me lots of questions with regard to my time as a Japanese prisoner of war and why it had been such a long time before making the journey back. She would compose an article which possibly might appear in the paper at a later date, but as a junior reporter a decision to do this depended on the editor; whether it did or not I never found out. It is my belief that former colonial countries who achieve independence, after a period of years are not really happy to dwell on the past. They might retain the relics of that past but in my opinion that is done purely for tourism purposes. I think (very understandable) that they would like to bury all detail of colonial rule. In the evening I spent a pleasant time in the Oriental club, enjoying a good meal and a pleasant chat with the chef, who assured me that he considered it an honour to cook for a pleasant elderly gentleman with such an interesting history! Conversations with other guests in the lounge were also of interest, they were from all parts of the world but in the main they were only using Singapore as a stopover for one or two days. I myself had a purpose to be in Singapore in that I wanted to get the feel of the place and recharge my memories from 64 years ago, but most of these other travellers, I suppose simply wanted a clean well-run city in which to break their journey. To me the glamour and mystery of the old Singapore had gone, it wasn't a place for a holiday, and tomorrow I would carry out the main purpose of my visit by visiting the Changi Chapel and Museum together with the Kranji military cemetery. So with a nightcap at the bar, then up to my room, admire the lights including the Singapore Eye, and so to bed! I was up nice and early the next morning and although I could get to the Changi area by bus or light railway I decided to go by taxi. On arrival I made my way first to the chapel, which is actually a reconstruction of the original chapel set up by Padre N. Duckworth outside Changi jail, and that is one which I remember from being a prisoner of war. If I remember rightly Duckworth was Padre to the Cambridgeshire Regiment and before the war, whilst at Cambridge, was the cox of the 1936 Cambridge boat race crew. Being the cox he was very short in stature, but when it came to dealing with the Japanese he was a giant! He organised the building and equipping of the chapel, great use was made of bamboo and religious items (i.e. communion vessels) were made from metal mess tins. I don't think the Japanese were very happy about the chapel being there, but to us it was a place where you could get away from the dreary life we were living, a place where we could think about home, friends who had passed on, and where we could pray for deliverance in the future, it was a place of hope. The reconstructed chapel together with the museum were situated some distance away from the original site, probably due to the old prison being reconstructed and that area being fenced off. I gathered from enquiries that the new prison was to be far more palatial than the old, presumably no more concrete beds and "hole in the floor" toilets, even so the official guide books make no mention of the prison or its whereabouts!

I had taken with me on my trip to the Far East, a scrapbook, in which I had posted details of my Army life, it being my intention to leave it for posterity at the Museum at Kanchanaburi (Bridge on the River Kwai), and this I showed to Robin Blackburn, the manager at the Museum. He understood my reason for wanting to take it to Thailand but suggested that I might like to pin something on his memorial wall. I was happy to do so by pinning one of the few postcards that I received from home, whilst at Changi in 1944, together with a message that I was back after 64 years, in very good health and more importantly a survivor. The museum was also very interesting as it contained a replica of one of the Changi jail cells, which were very small and meant originally for one prisoner but for the POWs it was 6 to the cell; in addition there was a display of artefacts made mainly out of bamboo and used by the prisoners. Whilst I was there quite a number of other visitors turned up, including Australians, and I got chatting to one or two of them. A Mr and Mrs Turner from New South Wales were very interested in my story, hardly believing that I was a former POW, and after a while the other visitors realising that they were in the presence of a survivor, joined us to hear my story. Unfortunately in doing so they had deserted the official guide, who definitely was not pleased, possibly he saw the end of the tour with tips ending abruptly! I gathered from Robin Blackburn that a long time had passed since an original POW had visited the museum and it was obvious from the visitors I had met that most of them were there to remember grandfathers. When I left to go by taxi onto the Kranji war memorial I was seen off by everyone giving me a wave and best wishes for my future, it made me feel a bit of a celebrity! The Kranji war memorial is situated just west of the road leading to the Johor Causeway and is dedicated to all the service personnel who died in the conflict with the Japanese, and of course that covers many nationalities. The memorial, itself an imposing concrete structure, stands at the top of a small hill with the military's cemetery spread below it. There are about 4000 marked graves, whilst the names of those whose bodies were not recovered are inscribed on the walls of the memorial. As I contemplated the stiff climb to the top of the hill I met another Australian visitor, a Mr Daniel, a much younger man than myself who lent me an arm for the walk; Mr Daniel I believe was a farmer from New South Wales and his mission at the Memorial was on behalf of a friend requiring information about a soldier named Reid, quite a coincidence, it being the name of my favourite nephew Kenneth. It seemed to me that the majority of the marked graves are Australian, understandable bearing in mind that the initial Japanese invasion of the island had occurred on the western side of the island. The roughly 25,000 names inscribed on the memorial's walls are probably of those whose bodies were not recovered from the Malayan Peninsula. I was interested in those names relating to the 18th division, in particular the Royal Artillery, and I'm glad to say Mr Daniel found the grave he was looking for. The memorial and cemetery are beautifully laid out, the trees and flowers are outstanding but of course being in Singapore you wouldn't expect anything else, since everything in Singapore is neat, tidy and impeccably clean, the regime in the country is strict in these matters but there is no doubt that it puts the untidiness in some parts of our country to shame.

After our visit my new found friend and I caught a taxi back to town and he very kindly treated me to a meal at his hotel, and so ended the day, full of memories for me and a renewal of my friendship for Australians; good on you, cobbers! The next day I decided for the main part to take it easy, I had done a fair bit of walking the previous day and so after a late breakfast I explored the shopping malls and marvelled at the displays in the shops. Prices, especially of jewellery, watches and electrical goods seemed remarkably low, mostly imports from Japan, how ironic! In the early afternoon I went to the Esplanade Theatre on the Bay for a cafe lunch and to listen to the orchestra playing on the stage. The audience was mainly young people chatting away and enjoying their sandwiches. It was very informal with everyone happy with life, lots of laughter and amongst it all I felt a bit of a dinosaur, it was so different from that time of long ago, maybe it was time to bury the past. Later that day, in the early evening, I decided to visit Raffles Hotel, which I knew was not too far away on the other side of the war memorial park, and on my way I admired an enormous bronze statue of a bull on a large plinth, but as I couldn't see any inscription on the sculpture I can only assume it was a piece of modern street art. I entered the hotel up the marble steps past the uniformed Sikh doorman and went into the foyer and found that the old long bar was no longer there. Apparently it had become so popular with tourists wishing to imbibe in Singapore gin slings that it had been recreated in an annex attached to the hotel; this piece of information destroyed for me all the ambience of the place. On one side of the foyer a tearoom had been set up, again to allow tourists to participate in afternoon tea at Raffles, but of course at a price and booking in advance, the old days had certainly gone! However I sauntered over to a small bar set up in the opposite corner and in doing so passed an American gentleman tinkling on a grand piano; (shades of Casablanca!) the tune was familiar to me as an old Army one, the words of which runs as follows "When this ****ing war is over; oh so happy I shall be; when I get my civy clothes on; no more soldiering for me; no reveille in the morning; no more polishing my brass; I can tell the sergeant major; to stick his rifle up his a***. On passing this piece of knowledge to him he replied that he had always regarded the piece of music as a hymn tune, thanked me and played a reprise for my benefit. I carried on to the bar where I spent a pleasant half-hour chatting to the barman over a couple of beers, following which I made my way past the pianist, (who played my tune as I went by), out to the front steps, where I promptly slipped and fell. To the astonishment of the resplendent uniformed Sikh, and for that matter myself, I landed backwards onto a large earthen ornamental pot complete with small palm, all of which disintegrated under my weight. I was helped to my feet by the 6'6" doorman who was very concerned, especially when he observed that my bush shirt was torn and there was a slight trickle of blood on my back. The assistant manager was called who insisted that I should rest in the lounge and brought me a stiff drink; my shirt was removed and the Sikh produced a first aid box and applied a liberal dose of iodine. As far as I was concerned it was just a scratch and I felt fine; I was worried about the pot plant, but possibly the hotel management was worried about a legal suit in the offing. In due course a taxi was called to convey me back to the Mandarin Oriental, who were informed by telephone to expect me. As I made my way to the taxi from the lounge, through the foyer accompanied by the management and of course my friend the Sikh, we went by my other friend the pianist and I couldn't resist saying "play it again Sam" which he did. I left Raffles hotel singing my old Army ditty, it made my day! On arrival at the Mandarin Oriental I was greeted almost as a hero, again by an assistant manager, the doorman and a couple of members of the staff. Apparently I was famous for smashing up a rival hotel's ornamental pot, I was notorious! Back in my own room I had a shower, put a new plaster on my scratch, went down dressed for dinner to the Oriental club had a good meal with a bottle of wine, and so to bed, ready for the next day when I would be on my way to Thailand.

The next morning two messages were delivered to me before breakfast, the first from the hotel deputy manager letting me know that Raffles hotel had enquired that morning as to my health, and assurance had been given that I was fighting fit. The second message concerned my trip on the Eastern and Oriental Express, apparently there had been a serious accident on the railway line in Malaya which had delayed the south bound Express. This meant a delay in cleaning and preparing the train for its return journey so therefore our departure due just after 11 a.m. would be delayed. I was informed that I would not be picked up until 3.45 p.m., then would be taken to the Regent Hotel to rendezvous with all the other travellers. We were given a meal at the hotel, later taken to Keppel Road station for boarding the train at 6 p.m., eventually departing at 6.30 p.m. At the station the Oriental express awaited us. I was shown in to my Pullman compartment by a young Malay steward, who demonstrated how everything worked, assuring me that he was available at any time on the press of a button, at the same time telling me his name, which being impossible to repeat I shortened to Monty.

The decor of the train was magnificent, my luggage had been handled for me at every stage of my journey from Glasgow, and again now sat ready for me in my compartment. Owing to the rail accident the itinerary of the journey was altered, a short daylight stop at Kuala Lumpur was not possible (we passed it during the night), but we had the next day a longer visit to explore Penang. After settling down we were called to dinner and in view of the late departure the dress code was slightly relaxed; the food was splendid, a gastronomic delight, and soon there was a lively conversation with table companions (two from England and one from Canada). For future meals I discovered that table companions were always changed and obviously this led to everyone getting to know their fellow travellers, who were from all parts of the world. Following dinner I explored the rest of the train, there was a reading room, a lounge bar with a resident pianist and at the rear of the train an observation car, and for the ladies there was even a boutique. On returning to my cabin I found that Monty had transformed the compartment to a bedroom complete with fruit and flowers, however not being ready for bed, I hot footed it along to the bar for my usual night cap and a chat with fellow travellers, most of them were intrigued by my age and the reason for my visit to Thailand. Eventually I retired to bed, a tired old soldier; Monty called for any last-minute request, a pot of tea perhaps? Maybe a final nightcap? No thank you, just a quick shower and so to bed. Before I drifted into sleep I went back in my mind to that time in 1943, when I stretched out on the metal floor of the truck with my fellow

POWs, on that journey to the Kwai; this time the journey would help to erase that memory, at least I hope so. I dropped off to sleep pretty quickly, despite the rumble of the train, but I think it must have been in the early hours of the morning when I was aware of lights and noise outside the train which was stationary. We were in Kuala Lumpur station for a short time, but being very comfortable, I stayed in bed and dropped off to sleep. I woke about 7 a.m. aware of a smiling face looking down at me, "Mister Ransom Sir you like tea"? Following a shower, Monty again turned up requesting my requirements for breakfast, which was duly served in my compartment. Exploration of the train followed; to the rear I found the observation car and I was able to appreciate in the warm air, the luxuriant scenery passing by, accompanied of course by a cooling drink; it was not like that the last time! In the other direction from my compartment lay the reading room with the day's newspapers, the dining rooms and the lounge where following my time in the observation car I enjoyed a pre-lunch beverage. On my way back from the observation car I noted that my bedroom was now a lounge, well done Monty!

Lunch was a splendid affair, the cuisine out of this world and the company again of three different fellow travellers. It was not long after lunch that we pulled into Butterworth, where we alighted and boarded coaches to take us on to the ferry, across to Penang and into the capital George Town. After Singapore, Penang with its harbour and defences was a vital cog in the war against the Japanese. In fact it had been a one of the oldest settlements being founded by Sir Stamford Raffles prior to Singapore. Unfortunately in the early part of the war it had been evacuated by the British and left more or less to its own devices, with the military believing that the civilians left behind would be treated reasonably well. However, the Chinese being in a predominantly Malay area suffered badly, hundreds of them being executed, causing great bitterness at that time. The radio station had been left untouched and was used to broadcast propaganda to the Indian troops and the Malay population. In addition, small craft left in the harbour were used by the Japanese in their landings further down the coast, to bypass mainly Australian troops. Penang and George Town in the old days were jewels in the crown of the British Empire; it was interesting now to see it as one of the principal areas of an independent Malaysia. On alighting from the coach in George Town we were organised on to rickshaws, it was great fun and a novel way to see the sights. The traffic was extremely busy and my heart was in my mouth as my chap between the shafts, weaved his way along the streets, all the time giving a running commentary on the sites we were passing I missed a great deal of the chat preferring to give my attention to possible disasters. Later on towards the end of the tour rivalry developed between the rickshaws resulting in heartrending manoeuvres. The scenery and the old world charm of the town was marvellous, but I was glad and relieved to finally get back to the coach, the ferry, and home to the train.

Back in my compartment I had time to spare to take it easy, with Monty duly supplying a pot of tea, then in due course, a shower followed to freshen up for dinner. This meal, we had been promised, would be the highlight of the trip, so naturally out came my dinner suit, with yours truly making every effort to look spic and span and if possible a little younger than my age. Again I had three different companions at the table, two Americans and one from New Zealand and as you can guess the conversation was stimulating and interesting. As the next morning would see our visit to the Bridge on the Kwai naturally, questions were aimed at me, as by this time all the passengers on the train were aware, that in my case, the visit to the Kwai was the principal reason for my being with them. The food, the wine and the service was out of this world. I don't think I have ever enjoyed anything better and probably never will. After dinner nearly everyone made their way to the Bar Car with its sumptuous seating, decor and service provided by waitresses in their national costume. Music was supplied by a pianist (who from his accent probably originated from London) playing old and new popular tunes, but later when drink flowed and people mingled and the evening wore on, life for me became a little hazy. Of course I stood my hand as regards drinks, but quite a quantity of alcohol seemed to have been provided for me! Later I dimly recalled leading everyone in singing "I belong to Glasgow" and "I love London town", songs which the pianist managed to thump out but which were followed with difficulty by some of the cosmopolitan gathering. I have photographs which indicate that at some stage in the proceedings I danced with the Thai waitresses in their costumes, I remember vaguely that earlier in the evening they had given a display of typical Thai dancing, with its slow deliberate movements, but what kind of dance I did later, I can't imagine. The Eastern and Oriental express company in their booklet had stated that although food service ceased at a certain hour, the Bar Car which opened at 08:00 hours could stay open as long as needed, in my opinion along with my fellow travellers I would say this was an extremely sensible decision!

It was late (actually early morning) when I got back to my compartment, again already turned by Monty and his magic wand into a bedroom, thank God. I quickly lost consciousness. The next morning Monty woke me up (with difficulty) with the usual revival cup of tea and following breakfast I made my way to the observation car to view in comfort the passing scenery.

At some time in the previous evening we had crossed the border into Thailand from Malaya and as our passports had been collected in advance by the stewards, we had not been bothered by any formalities. We were now beginning to travel along the Kra Isthmus and in the main the view to either side of the line consisted of paddy fields, this was the country's rice bowl. We were now approaching Kanchanaburi, which for tourists was the site of the "Bridge on the River Kwai" and I was surprised to receive a message from the train manager to the effect that I was not to go with the main party but that the manager of the Kwai Museum would himself pick me up to take me on a personal tour of the site; apparently nowadays they rarely received a visit from an original POW. Sure enough when the train pulled in at the Bridge I was greeted by Rod Beattie who was the curator of the Thailand – Burma Railway Museum and taken by him for a tour of the museum and introduced to his colleague Andrew Snow. Over a cup of tea we had a great discussion about the railway and all those who were concerned in its building; I was surprised to learn that Rod had spent more than 14 years researching the full story regarding the railway and had covered all aspects of its building with its cost in human life.

The exhibits in the museum were comprehensive and I was pleased to see several drawings done by my old friend Jack Chalker displayed on a wall, of course there were numerous artefacts that had been recovered from the railway, which Rod during the 14 years had amassed. Rod, quite rightly, emphasises in the museum the fiction of the movie "the Bridge on the River Kwai" which quite frankly, as every former POW knows, was a load of rubbish. In truth there is no bridge over the Kwai, in fact there was no river of that name. After the railway reached Kanchanaburi it required the first bridge to be built over the river Maeklaung following which, the path of the railway met the river Khwae Noi and followed the eastern bank of that river all the way to the Burmese border. Therefore there were no bridges over the Khwae Noi (Kwai as in the movie), but simply numerous small trestle bridges over streams running into the main river. However near the Burmese border, just below the camp where I myself had been, was the infamous No 2 Camp where the railway crossed a main tributary, which had required the building of a large trestle bridge. This Camp and the work carried on from it resulted in the deaths of over 1000 men, and it may be that its story is the origin of the book on which the movie is based, but of course this camp is well over 200 km upcountry from the tourist bridge! The cemetery at Kanchanaburi is well cared for and contains the remains of about 7000 Allied servicemen (mainly reburied after recovery from camps along the railway) and in addition there are cemeteries at Chungkai (10 km upstream) and at Thanbyuzayat in Burma. Of course many burials, especially in small camps, were never found and I believe that those with no known grave are recorded at the military cemetery in Singapore. I had hoped to see the grave of a fellow sergeant of my regiment, namely Ron Breacker, who was dying when I left the camp near the Three Pagodas pass, but I learned that those POWs who had died in the camps near the Burma border had in fact been taken and reburied in the Burma cemetery.

As a result of my visit, Andrew Snow, an assistant at the Museum, kindly sent me a list of all the men of 118 Field Regiment who had died either in Thailand or on prison ships going to Japan. During the building of the railway, except for a short period at Kanchanaburi, I had spent my time at the camp at Kami Sonkurai and until I met Rod Beattie my knowledge of the other camps was limited. Before I left to return to the train Rod presented me with a copy of his book which had not long been published, entitled "The Death Railway" kindly inscribed by himself. Only a small portion of the railway now exists as the jungle has swallowed up most of it and in addition a large area has been used to create a reservoir. Luckily Rod Beattie has recovered quite a large amount of artefacts now on show in the museum and I was extremely pleased when as well as his book, he gave me a railway spike he had recovered from the jungle; it now makes a great paperweight! I showed Rod my personal scrapbook which showed my Army life from being a territorial up to my final release, including all related documents, and more importantly all communications between myself and home whilst a POW (these were not many and came to exist all towards the end of the war). In view of my age and with no family of my own, I offered the scrapbook to Rod for the museum and I was very pleased when he expressed his delight in receiving it. Later Rod took me back to the train and on the short drive I looked around me, after all the years it was so different from what I remembered, it was now a modern town, not as before, a collection of nondescript dwellings on a dusty road. In my mind I tried to bring back the memory of the old prisoner of war camp, all the dust after the monsoon, the bamboo huts with their atap roofs and its overall appearance of a refugee camp. In spite of its misery I remember it as a place where I first received news of home and from that point of view it was a damn site better than the camp up near Three Pagodas, and also the food was very slightly better. To get to the Bridge the train had left the Singapore to Bangkok mainline on a branch spur which required the engine to be brought to the other end of the train, a manoeuvre which puzzled most of the passengers on the final stage of the journey, many going in the wrong direction for lunch! In two or three hours we would be in Bangkok and over lunch many of my fellow travellers were interested to know how I felt about going back to the Kwai after so many years; they of course were of different generations and to them the Bridge was simply a tourist attraction, for me it took me back to my youth. As in the title of an old song it was "a sentimental journey", it was worth every penny to go back and see it all again, to say goodbye to old comrades, and in a way to enjoy a sense of satisfaction that I had beaten the odds and survived to a ripe old age. I felt like singing another song, the old Army one "Bless them all". If you have been in the Services you will know all the words, if not it is suffice for me to say that the song indicates the end of military life. After lunch there was only an hour or two before we arrived in Bangkok so I made myself comfortable in the observation car and watched the countryside go past. In the main it was paddy field after paddy field, with the occasional collection of wooden houses, also now and then a domed temple. We were not travelling at great speed and those workers beside the track or in the fields always stopped to give us a friendly wave, and of course we reciprocated.

Eventually we pulled into Hualampong station in Bangkok just before 3 p.m. where we disembarked, with a car taking me to my hotel for my stay until Tuesday. On the train I had been well looked after by Monty and we said our goodbyes as if we had been friends for years; also as we dispersed, best wishes were given to fellow travellers as we made our way down the platform. We were not burdened with luggage, it had already been taken off the train and placed in the appropriate cars from the hotels. All the staff from the train were lined up to give us a farewell wave, I think we all felt like royalty. For me this had been the end of an epic journey, it had replaced in my mind, the one of 1943, one more bogey laid to rest.

I shall always remember with fondness my stay in the Oriental Bangkok, a hotel with 130 years of history situated on the banks of Bangkok's River of King's. On arrival I was greeted with smiles and during my short stay friendliness abounded creating an atmosphere which seemed to rub off on to guests. After checking in, a member of staff stepped forward and announced in stentorian tones that he was my butler and was there to solve any problem that may arise (shades of Ali Baba, your wish, is my command). Well I was in the Far East! After settling down in my very comfortable room I took time to explore the magnificent hotel which prides itself on being one of the best in the world, which I can well believe. On taking afternoon tea in the splendid entrance lobby I was intrigued by the manner in which it was served by the waitress in Thai costume; she approached the low table with a large tray, sank quite effortless onto her knees to pour the tea, apparently when serving, a servant's head should not be higher than that of the guest, quite a difficult move with the guest sprawled on a low divan! It made my knees ache watching the lass! As had happened at the Singapore hotel, the staff in Bangkok seem to be aware that they were dealing with a very old soldier and accordingly made every effort to look after me, but somehow here in Thailand there was that little extra in smiles and charm. I think that the Thai people must be one of the friendliest nations in the world. The hotel had quite a number of restaurants specialising in types of Oriental cooking and in addition French cuisine, Italian fare and of course seafood specialities. As far as I was concerned elaborate meals late at night at my age would be asking for trouble therefore I took an early evening meal in The Verandah restaurant which was ideal for my modest requirements. During the day afternoon tea could also be taken in the Authors' Lounge, a room preserved from the old days when it was frequented by such as Somerset Maugham and Joseph Conrad. After my evening meal it was my want during my stay to frequent the Bamboo Bar, the hotel's famous rendezvous where one could meet and chat with fellow travellers.

I spent the day after my arrival taking trips from the hotel's private landing stage, exploring the river and in particular the shopping complex known as River City, and it was in the vicinity of this area, whilst enjoying a coffee, that I met a most remarkable woman. Henny Schoute-Bussolati was enjoying a coffee at the next table on the veranda of the small cafe in the square. Hearing my English accent when I ordered my coffee, she enquired if I was on holiday. After the usual chat about the weather we got round to the purpose of my visit to Thailand and like most people that I had met she was surprised that a fellow of my age should have been undertaking a "journey of remembrance" after such a long period of time. Naturally we both got reminiscing about the old days and if I thought my story was one worth telling then it did not in any way surpass Henny's history. In 1966 she had gone as the first Dutch female war correspondent to Vietnam, subsequently serving for five years in medical clinics attached to the American forces, and apparently this had involved making parachute jumps over Vietnam and Laos. Her subsequent marriage to an American was followed by divorce and Henny resumed her career as a foreign correspondent in the USA, the Lebanon and Fiji, before returning to the Netherlands. Finally her health began to deteriorate and she went back to Fiji where the more agreeable and warmer climate would be helpful but when I met her she had returned to Southeast Asia. I gathered that despite her failing health she is still trying to convey and bring about more awareness of the aftermath of the war and the use of the chemical agent Orange, an agent which was probably one of the reasons for her own ill-health. When we finally parted on that Sunday (11 October 2009) we exchanged addresses, and I suppose we both felt a degree of satisfaction at having met another "old soldier" with whom to share the past, mind you Henny's story took some beating!

That night I sat in the Bamboo bar over a couple of beers thinking about the day and I wondered if those writers in the past, who stayed at the Oriental Hotel years ago, received inspiration for their stories from incidents which happened to them during their visits to Bangkok. I was just on my second beer when Graham walked in, ordered a beer and started chatting; as usual, an enquiry "why was an old chap alone in Bangkok" and of course out came my story! Graham LaCourt worked for an American company specialising in hydrocarbons and looked after their offices in Shanghai and presumably Bangkok. He was extremely interested in my story about the

Thai – Burma railway and could hardly believe that I had returned after all those years to visit the Kwai again. He appeared to have houses in Bangkok and Shanghai and he was married to a young Vietnamese girl who looked after the Bangkok house together with her father. Graham (who appeared to be middle-aged) seemed very happy with life and the arrangement which enabled him to leave his Bangkok house in safe hands whilst in Shanghai, why not? He suggested that since he had the next day free he would show me the town, an offer I was happy to accept since I reasoned that if he lived there he would know his way around and so arrangements were made to meet the next morning at 11 a.m. Where? Of course in the Bamboo bar! Promptly the next day Graham turned up and off we went, and Graham certainly showed me Bangkok! We hopped off and on river taxis, explored side streets and saw parts of Bangkok which I'm sure the ordinary tourist would never see. We had at least four stops at pavement cafes, ate peculiar local snacks, washed down with local beers, and in one instance even had local firewater to drink. We had started off at 11 a.m and six hours later I was at the end of my tether, my feet were on fire. Graham, although he would not admit it, I felt sure was just as exhausted, suggested we would call in for a massage. Noting my hesitation he made it clear that it was our feet that would receive attention, and so we entered the appropriate establishment to be received by some charming ladies. Each foot received 30 mins of pummelling with the use of oils and I must say at the end I felt a new man! Graham paid the bill which I understood was quite reasonable, and at the same time telling the girls my life story, the only part of which causing raised eyebrows, was my age. This I found flattering especially when all the staff appeared, amounting to 6 girls and a very sinister looking man, and insisted that we should be photographed with them outside the establishment. I have a feeling that a large copy of the photograph is now plastered on the wall of the establishment as a form of advertisement! I think it was about 8 p.m. when we, arrived back at the hotel, food we did not need, so we made our way of course to the Bamboo bar for further refreshment. The day was not over, we met three Americans and once again yours truly had to explain his presence in Thailand, and once again for the umpteenth time I was assured that I did not look my age, and in any case it was an excuse for a drink! The Americans appeared to be in their late 30s and were very interested in the Second World War and accordingly plied me with questions which in my befuddled state I endeavoured to answer to the best of my ability. One question seemed very important to them "in 1945 why did we give Churchill the boot?" Luckily I was able to point out that at the time of the election I was still in the custody of the Japanese. They had come across to the Bamboo bar from their hotel on the other side of the river and I found out that one of them was a politician who was being taken on holiday by the other two who were lawyers. We all got on splendidly together, more beer and a photograph taken, also arrangements were made by the Americans with Graham (who had my recommendation as a guide) for a little sightseeing in the future. The evening ended with us being all very good friends, lots of discussion on many subjects, and eventually the Americans went back across the river. Graham went back presumably to his wife and father-in-law and I myself went up to bed. Later when I got home I received a photograph and a communication from a politician who turned out to be Chris Koster, Attorney General of Missouri, and I'm pleased to say that we have been in communication from time to time since. The next day was spent recovering and doing a little shopping before catching a flight in the evening for Dubai, arriving there early on Wednesday to spend two days before departing early Friday for Glasgow. The time that I spent in Dubai was short and on reflection I felt that it had been a waste, it would have been better to have extended my stay in Bangkok (bearing in mind my activities in that city), and flown home from there. Dubai had none of the charm or interest of Bangkok, it was far too busy, too commercial and too brash for me, although the hotel itself (Hilton Dubai Creek) was very comfortable. I did a little sightseeing and in a way the old town with the trading junks tied up at the quayside was quite interesting, but a good part of the other areas of the town was still under development with many buildings needing completion and occupation. The airport was new and magnificent but it was also vast, I could have done with a mobile scooter getting around it. I was happy to get out of it when I arrived on the Wednesday and happier still on the Friday when I boarded my plane at about 8 a.m. to fly back to Glasgow. At my age I probably will not be going to the Far East again but if I do Dubai will be given a miss. The final leg of my journey was uneventful and it was just after midday when we touched down in Glasgow, but I am sorry to say that the efficiency and facilities that had been present at the airports abroad was not repeated in Glasgow. By comparison Glasgow was shabby with a lack of organisation, no luggage trolleys to be had, but I was happy now to be back, with my nephew Kenneth and his wife Elsa waiting to take me back to Cumbrae Court, Largs.

# MADDIE AND MARRIAGE

## Maddie and Marriage to present day

It did not take me long to settle down in my flat, and once I had done so I gave Maddie a ring to let her know that I was back. I could tell that she was pleased that I had quickly got in touch with her. In fact some months later she did confess her belief that maybe following my trip, I would not renew our relationship, silly woman! No, as far as I was concerned I was very anxious to see her again, as soon as possible. I arrived back in Largs on the Saturday and the next day I hot footed it up to number 3 Homemount, where of course I was made very welcome and naturally we had a lot to talk about. The once a week meetings at the Gypsy Cream for a bowl of soup still continued but now extra meetings were arranged by Maddie and I, with barely more than two days passing without us seeing each other, always at her flat as I think she was a bit shy at coming up to Cumbria Court. In some ways she was a little old-fashioned, on my visits to her flat she insisted that the time for my departure should coincide with the lighting of the street lamps going on! As it was now winter, early tea was followed by a swift goodbye! I suppose that since we were both residents in complexes for people over 60 it was essential to avoid any possible tittle-tattle, but I myself didn't care a jot! In November the reporter of the local newspaper realised that I had returned from the River Kwai and did a follow up from his first story. It was quite a good spread and included two of my photographs, one with me at the Changi Museum and the other in a lighter moment with me leering at a Thai girl on the Orient express! In a small place like Largs news travels fast and in months to follow I found myself roped in for lectures and talks at local organisations, such is fame! Mind you in a small town it's essential to lead a clean life!, no hint of scandal, otherwise no one wants to know you, and you are doomed! By Christmas I felt that again I should accept my nephew's invitation to join him and his family for a day or two although I did feel a little guilty about Maddie being on her own but she was adamant I should go. After the New Year, Maddie asked me to join her for a Burns night supper, to be held at her complex at Homemount. Years previous (in the 1950s) at Peebles I had attended a Burns night and if my memory serves me right it had been a rather solemn affair; this one turned out to be completely different, yes there were the usual rituals concerning the haggis, one or two ballads listened to with a reverence but after that the evening developed into what would be called in Del boy country, a bit of a "knees up". The music most of the time was of the popular variety (nothing to do with Burns and in most cases not even Scotland) and the dancing tended to be fast and furious, for over 60s it was remarkable! The manager of the complex and his wife were determined that all and sundry would have a night to remember and more or less threw themselves into the fray, the manager resplendent in tartan bonnet and yellow wig insisted on whirling senior ladies off the floor much to their delight! Maddie and I were more than a little surprised at the style of this Burns supper, we had gone soberly dressed, Maddie in a long skirt and tartan sash with myself wearing a tartan tie (borrowed off old Jock Morrison), in the appropriate Morrison tartan, bearing in mind its connection with the supermarket where I had first met Maddie. It was very late when I left to go back to my own flat, streetlights had been on quite a long time, but it had been a very enjoyable evening, spent in good company with someone who was beginning to be a major item in my life, what more could I wish for?

We were now moving towards my 90th birthday for which I had plans involving my two nephews and niece and their connection with my early days with Helen in Peebles. Of course I wanted Maddie to be a part of the celebration but as we were going as a party for a few days to the Park Hotel at Peebles she felt that she did not want to intrude on a family affair, bearing in mind that she had not yet met any of them. In fact Maddie was still steering clear of Cumbrae Court and I was reasonably sure that the inhabitants therein were not aware of our courting, of course I still joined the ladies on Thursday afternoons for tea. Entry to the complex was not easy (on a par with Fort Knox), as keys were needed for a pedestrian gate, with separate gates for cars, and at odd times visitors needed entry and my entry button seemed always to be the one they pressed. I am also pressed into service, resetting cookers after any power cut, with my advice being sought on many a domestic matter, and in fact I think I was regarded as Jim the manager's assistant, probably due in some part for our being engrossed from time to time with our football fixed odds discussions. However I suppose it's nice to be needed!

My 90th birthday celebration at Peebles was a most enjoyable occasion, my nephews and my niece and their partners booked in with me for three days at the Park Hotel and at dinner on 15 April 2010 we were joined by some local

Peeblians who I had known from the past. Among them was John McOwan a one-time jeweller in the high street, but now retired and almost as old as myself and likewise a widower. Our friends from those times after the war had all passed on, and he and I remembered with affection, Betty, David and Margaret, Harry and Lillian and of course my dear Helen. It was hard to believe that 70 years had passed since my army truck had pulled up that night in 1940 on the road outside, and it is difficult for me to account for the time that has gone by but I'm determined to have a good shot at it!

On getting back to Largs my love for Maddie deepened and hardly a day passed without us getting together, we had such a great deal in common, not least a sense of humour, and of course we were interested in each other's lives before we met. She had been born and lived as a child in Tignabruaich (I can spell it but now saying it, no way!) before moving to Dunoon. Since in that summer of 2010 it was advertised that the paddle steamer "Waverley" would be going there once a week until the end of August, we waited patiently for a good day, weather wise. All in vain, on every occasion the rain poured down, and the journey would not be made until the following year, in greatly altered circumstances. In April I had been advised by my optician to have a cataract operation on my left eye but of course there was the usual waiting-list with the possibility that the operation would not be done for five or six months. However I pointed out to my GP that, at the age of ninety delays involving any medical procedure would be asking for trouble, following which he pulled a few straws, and the operation was successfully done in early August. This unaccustomed brush with the medical profession gave me food for thought; perhaps action was needed before anything else needed repairing or maybe things might drop off! The autumn was coming and the daylight getting shorter, soon the street lamp lighting would mean an earlier curfew for me! There was only one thing to do, let's get married!

Luckily for me Maddie felt as I did, accepted my proposal and without further ado we sat down to make the arrangements. Initially we felt that we both needed a short holiday and accordingly we booked a few days break at Peebles (No, at our age it was not a trial run!), also inviting Maddie's friend Janet along with us. Unfortunately Janet had to return home on the second day due to her sister's serious illness and with Maddie not feeling very well on one or two of the days, the holiday break was not all that successful. As Janet's car was our means of transportation, we were rescued on the day of our departure by my two nephews, Andrew organising "Peebles to Glasgow" and Kenneth dealing with "Glasgow to Largs", and at the handover it felt like a consignment of goods transaction! Back at base, Maddie and I discussed wedding arrangements, and with Maddie not being 100% fit felt that we should consider, early in the next year, but thankfully I was able to persuade her that we should make the great day, before Christmas. The next four or five weeks were hectic, the actual day of the wedding was fixed for 25 November with the ceremony to be held at the Seamill Hydro in Ayrshire with a small gathering of friends and relations. The registrar was arranged, wedding cake ordered for delivery, overnight rooms at the Hydro booked, seating arrangements set and many other matters dealt with. Maddie initially had chosen Janet, whom she had known for many years, to be her matron of honour but unfortunately the illness of her sister required Janet's full-time attention, so accordingly Kenneth's wife Elsa stepped in as a replacement which was appropriate seeing that I had already arranged for Kenneth to be my best man. Maddie still had to find a wedding dress plus accessories and she was helped in this by the manager and his wife at Homemount, namely David and Mary who provided transport. We had decided that after the ceremony we would return straight back the next day to Cumbrae Court for a complete rest after such a hectic few weeks, leaving any arrangements for a honeymoon for the future! Of course the wedding arrangements needed both of us to make trips to the registrar's office in Largs, access to which is made through the medical centre and on the first occasion two Cumbrae Court residents sitting waiting to see the doctor, observed Maddie and I passing through, which gave rise to much speculation! On being quizzed later I denied ever being there and suggested that a visit to the optician was required! The registrar at Largs had hoped to conduct the ceremony at Seamill Hydro as she was delighted and interested in our story but unfortunately she could not do this as she was due to retire a week before the day, a North Ayrshire colleague would step in. No matter, we invited her as a guest.

The guest list was under 20 in number, Maddie's sister Euphie of course, my nephews and niece with their partners and other friends, most of us gathering together at the Hydro the day before for a very sociable get-together. Needless to say there was a late-night party in Ken and Elsa's room ( I think) where amongst other beverages a superb bottle of German brandy was consumed, the donor of which (Euphie's friend John) unfortunately missed out on; he has since forgiven us! It was late when I finally made my way up to my room on the top floor. Maddie insisted that decorum would be followed from start to finish in our courtship, everything needed to be signed, sealed and delivered! The wedding day weather was beautiful, the November day was like a summers day, blue skies with the blue water stretching over to the Isle of Arran, calm and sparkly. After breakfast the lads (me too) went down to the beach for a breath of fresh air, the ladies besieging the hairdressing salon. About 1.30 p.m. I went upstairs to get formally dressed and during this process, standing in my underwear, I reached into the wardrobe for my white dress shirt, oh hell it wasn't there! Then I remembered, I had kept it separate (to avoid creasing) in my wardrobe at Cumbrae Court, after putting in cufflinks. Immediately I made a phone call to the hotel manager for help, but no luck so hastily donning a pair of slacks, shot down to Ken and Elsa's room where both were also beginning to get dressed for the ceremony. Ken did not have a spare shirt, just the fresh white one he had that moment put on, but without hesitation he pulled it off and handed it to me (luckily we both took the same neck size) and before he changed his mind I belted back to the attic. Later on when he was standing by my side, I had a peep at him in his light cream, slightly crumpled, shirt which I understood he had worn for his journey the day before, but personally I thought he looked quite dapper in it! The time for the "off" was 2.30 p.m. which I made breathlessly with a minute to spare but I need not have rushed, as the hotel manager had discovered that two guests were missing and it was some minutes before it was discovered that a message left in the hairdressing salon had not been passed on. Apparently a friend of Maddie had phoned to say her husband had been indisposed and could not travel, and in the meanwhile Maddie and Elsa were told to wait in the bridal suite until everything had been sorted out, and naturally by this time Maddie's nerves were a little bit shattered!

Eventually with Ken and I in place Maddie and Elsa appeared and Maddie was absolutely beautiful in her off the shoulder Chinese silk dress, and Elsa didn't look bad either. The window behind the registrar framed a magnificent view of Arran across the water, the sun shone and as far as I was concerned all was well in the world. At the age of ninety, in good health, I was a very lucky man. After the ceremony we all made our way to a small lounge whilst the reception room was rearranged for the wedding meal, and over a champagne toast our guests wished us good luck for the future and very kindly complimented us on our appearance. Apparently we were beautiful and didn't look our ages, yes, those that needed them did wear glasses! The meal was excellent, speeches and toasts were made, Alistair, the husband of my niece Isabel, acted as photographer and finally in the early evening we made our way to the lounge bar which had been set aside for us. At the end of the day Maddie and I made our way to the bridal suite and at long last there was no need for me to depart when the street lamps went out! Needless to say we both had a sound sleep, the day had been tiring and of course we were not spring chickens! However we were up reasonably early the next morning to see off our friends who had also stayed overnight, and thinking back, this would appear to be contrary to tradition, normally the guests would see the bride and groom departing. Overnight the brilliant sunny weather had departed, the skies were now overcast, snow had fallen during the night and was still falling, and one by one our friends left and as we learned later some had difficulty in getting home as most of Scotland was subject to a blizzard which lasted for some time. Maddie and I got back to Largs about midday, calling at Morrisons Supermarket (where else!) for provisions before reaching our flat which to our surprise was festooned with balloons, streamers and messages of goodwill. As far as I can remember I made no attempt to carry Maddie over the threshold but I would hasten to say this was due to my lack of strength rather Maddie's weight! Number 3 Cumbrae Court was no longer a bachelor pad but from the 26th November 2010 to the present day, when we are now past our second wedding anniversary, it has been a very happy home for both of us.

My trip back to the Kwai in 2009 had attracted the attention of the local newspaper so it was not very long before my marriage activity also received publicity, and an article duly appeared, emphasising our ages ( the repetition goes on and on!) with a large heading "They met in supermarket checkout". Maddie was not too pleased with this especially as the article ended with the comment that "love can be found even in the fruit and vegetable aisle" but I laughed my head off! In the summer of 2011 we had our long awaited honeymoon, and as an elderly couple we settled for a cruise and as the Fred Olsen line were operating from Greenock, only a few miles away, we chose a Mediterranean cruise aboard the Boadicea. We were fortunate in that after booking a main deck cabin we were upgraded twice and found ourselves in a palatial suite four decks higher; needless to say our happiness was complete.

In 2012 the London Olympics passed by and even those awakened once again my memories. Events were held in Greenwich Park Royal artillery garrison at Woolwich, the millennium dome (02) and the area of Hackney marshes. My mind goes way back to Fred and I playing as young boys in the park, my sitting in the NAAFI canteen at Woolwich listening to Chamberlain declaring war, my grandfather tying up his barge at the old coal wharf and the odd football match I played in on the Marsh. I find it hard to believe now that I am 93 years of age, where have all the years gone, did I waste any? What about regrets? Did I always act kindly to my first love, dearest Helen, and to Joyce who gave me love and passion, when it was needed. Now at last, probably with not many years to go I have found peace and tranquillity with Maddie, I am a very lucky fellow. What do I hope for in the future? Well I would like to reach the age of a hundred with Maddie still with me, surely that's not too much to ask for? And if my present good health still holds then that would be a bonus. I would finally like to make one observation; my love for Scotland and the Scottish people has no bounds, I know I was born in Del boy country but believe me at heart I am Scots, providing you turn down the volume of the bagpipes! Well it is now the year 2013, and Maddie and I have been together for well over two years, and you may ask what has happened since our wedding? The answer could be "not a lot" but that would not be strictly true. Outsiders might consider we lead a humdrum life, but far from it, never have I been happier and I am sure that goes for Maddie. At our ages we are reasonably healthy, some aches and pains of course but looking forward to many years together. From time to time Ken and Elsa visit and keep us up to date with their family news, and at present their sons are spending their gap years in Australia. Maddie's friend Janet also from time to time looks in, and following the death of her sister which occurred shortly after our wedding, Janet has acted as guardian to her sisters three children, quite a task! I still think of the friends I made during my trip to the Far East in 2009, and in fact I still correspond with the Attorney General of Missouri, Chris Koster. Chris stood for re-election in 2012 as a Democrat and won through, and in the last communication from him he seems to be looking forward to 2016 when he hopes to stand for Governor. I replied, giving him my best wishes, pointing out that he could go further in 2020 when I could send him further congratulations coinciding with my 100th birthday! Of course Maddie will then be 89, we the Darby and Joan of Largs. As far as I'm concerned I'm in the country I love, with friends I love and with Maddie, the lady I love.

# Epilogue

We are now well into the year 2013 and the story of my life, so far, has been told. The story has covered a period of 93 years and on looking back I suppose it had its sorrow, tears and hardship but it also had many moments of pleasure, laughter and happiness. I cannot forget Helen and Joyce, they were partners on my life's journey and it now remains for me to contemplate what lies ahead. Whatever years are left for me, I am lucky that I can share them with Maddie here in Scotland. I love this country and its people, I feel that the Scots I have met have accepted me as a friend which accounts for the title of my book, truly I am a Scottish Cockney. In the political climate of today I have just one observation, the Scottish National party have done and are doing many things for the good of Scotland, maybe I will join the party providing they drop their desire for partition and simply be satisfied with achieving more jurisdiction over Scotland's affairs. My acceptance into the S.N.P. should follow, my having married two Scottish women, been employed by a Scottish company, been secretary of a Scottish football team and having lived in Scotland for a considerably long-time, what else can I do? Oh! I forget, my mother was a "Carr" which I believe or hope enables me to wear the Kerr tartan. Even now at my age life continues to be of interest, only a month or two ago I received a communication regarding Chris Koster, my old friend the Attorney General of Missouri. He had been re-elected in the recent American elections and was looking forward to 2016 when he hoped to stand for Governor of the State. I was happy to advise him to look even further to 2020 when perhaps he might reach even more dizzy heights! By that time I would be 100 years old and happy to receive an additional telegram along with the one from the Queen!